THE
ART
OF
BODY
SINGING

CREATE YOUR OWN VOICE

COMPLETE SERIES
VOLUMES I–IV
ALL LEVELS

by
Breck
Alan

Dedicated to Robert Cord

Produced by Breck Alan
Executive Produced by Wendy Rubin
Recorded and engineered by Breck Alan at Your Voice Vocal Studio, Austin, Texas
(with borrowed equipment from Charles Reeves & Scottie Closter)
Sound recording edited by Charles Reeves & Breck Alan at Chicky's, Austin Texas
Text edited by Troy Reust, Bethany Siegler & Wendy Rubin; book design/layout by Wendy Rubin
Illustrations by Peggy Pellett; pg. 70 postcard designs by Robin Borgers
Cover concept by Breck Alan; Cover illustration by Erica Vhay
Photography by Wendy Rubin
Additional graphic design by Lindsay Holmes
Segues *Airport Jive*, *Circus Trip*, *Weird Rain* & *Tiny's Tim* written by Charles Reeves and Breck Alan ©1996
All song examples in "The Art of Body Singing" written by Breck Alan
The Art of Body Singing, Volumes 1–4 text and recorded material written by Breck Alan, ©1997
The title "The Art of Body Singing"™ Breck Alan

for more information about The Art of Body Singing, please visit:
http://www.bodysinging.com

To contact Breck for private lessons, lectures and master classes:
breck@breckalan.com
1.888.563.7474 (1.888.joesgrille)
Or send inquiries to:
Breck Alan
P.O. Box 2380
New York, NY 10009

For information about Breck Alan as Artist (performance dates, CDs for sale, etc) please visit:
http://www.breckalan.com

Second Printing
Published By Breck Alan Music/Snacky Time Records, New York, NY
Volumes 1-4 ISBN 0-9705382-2-7
Library of Congress Control Number: 2001118606

Contents
Create Your Own Voice: Volumes I– IV

VOLUME III

VOLUME IV

THE
ART
OF
BODY
SINGING

CREATE YOUR OWN VOICE
VOLUME I

by
Breck
Alan

Introduction

The Art of Body Singing treats the serious student of voice to a meticulous, well organized journey, centered around the mechanics and techniques necessary in high performance singing. Body Singing adheres to the same essentials that any fine instrument-maker swears by: high quality design, high quality materials, and high quality assembly. Thus, the first concept of Body Singing: the voice is an instrument, assembly required. The system offers a methodical approach to vocal training, incorporating both classical and contemporary techniques. It is designed to teach proper vocal hygiene, high performance singing skills, personal style development and a professional outlook for ongoing growth long after leaving the teacher's side.

Most systems of vocal training, both historically and currently, are oriented in a coaching fashion, where students begin singing right away and are given only the vaguest tips on how to improve technically. And while there can certainly be a lot to learn from a coaching situation, i.e. repertoire training, sight reading, performance skills etc., these subjects can not be compared to vocal mechanics training. In the past, the only place to get really decent vocal mechanics training was from a good opera program. The drawback being you received training via a style, and that usually meant no matter what type of music you might later sing, you would probably sound like an opera singer trying to sing something else.

So what's the answer? The answer is a high level system of vocal training based on technique and not style. A system based on the ear as the first component of the voice, and then linking the ear to the series of physical feelings connected with producing sound from the body. The result being your own personal style of singing vs. singing on auto-pilot using muscle memory or pure imitation as the outcome of song coaching.

There is a lot of information and mis-information in the world concerning voice production. I have personally trained with some of the best vocal trainers, and some of the worst. I have spent countless hours with the more notorious published systems of voice as well as some of the least noteworthy. I have spent many a late night experimenting with techniques in search of that "Holy Grail Tone." So, after twelve years of singing, both as a student and as a professional, I set out to structure a system for vocal training. I truly wanted to create a balanced system incorporating the most effective information I had learned or discovered along my journey. Over five years later, the result is *The Art of Body Singing*. My belief is that I can literally save a student several years in their attempts to clear-ly understand the instrument called voice.

I must also credit my experience in the martial arts as much of my influ-ence in structuring *The Art of Body Singing*. Good martial arts' systems are taught from the ground up and add bit by bit to a solid foundation of learning. *The Art of Body Singing* borrows this systematic method of teaching and is designed for all levels of singers. Beginners will enjoy the fact that *The Art of Body Singing* starts literally at the beginning and clearly outlines how the instrument works in every-day terminology. Advanced singers will be ecstatic as they discover clear answers to the often glossed over questions of voice, while learning to use effective tools to conquer the brick walls they often come up against when trying to improve.

The voice like any other instrument is a lifelong pursuit; *The Art of Body Singing* will be an ongoing source of inspiration and information unlike any other in this world.

Truly Yours,

Breck Alan

THE
ART
OF
BODY
SINGING

CREATE YOUR OWN VOICE
VOLUME I

INTRODUCTION TO VOLUME 1

Welcome to *The Art of Body Singing*. No matter what level of singer you are, this is where you want to begin with this program. If you have some experience, you may find yourself working quickly through the first two volumes. However, these are necessary volumes to establish the vocabulary and foundation to move on in this system we call "Body Singing." Ideally, you should work one subject at a time, first listening to the recorded program then reviewing that subject in the booklet. The two mediums have been created to compliment each other in this program and, when used together, should prove to be frightfully effective. Don't work too quickly. Stay on each subject until you feel that you have grasped its full purpose, and have memorized the exercise so that you can practice it without the accompaniment of the recording or an instrument.

One of the goals of this system is to teach your voice to become a self-sufficient, freestanding instrument. It might help you at first to make a separate tape of just the exercises from "Body Singing" in the order that they appear, so that you might have a quick reminder of how they sound for your practice and warm-up sessions. Due to the amount of information covered in *The Art of Body Singing*, the recorded examples are not as long as you'll want them to be for your practice and warm-ups. So just use them as your starting examples, stop the recording, and commit them to memory. It is also likely that the starting notes for many of these exercises won't be a perfect fit for everyone. Once again, just use the example to learn the exercise then move the starting note to a more comfortable position. There might be times when it will be easier for women to learn the exercise from the men's example (following along an octave higher) and for men to learn from the woman's example (following along an octave lower). If this is difficult for you to do at first, ask someone (a musician friend or a music teacher) to help you figure it out. Once you understand how to move one or two of the exercises, custom fitting the rest of them shouldn't be a problem.

The voice is an instrument, an acoustic instrument to be exact. And like any other acoustic instrument, the voice has very specific physical properties that make it tick. What is unique to the voice is that you cannot buy it off the shelf like any other instrument you wish to play, but must instead build the instrument yourself. The voice can not be explained so simply as "being a muscle that gets stronger the more it is used." The voice is not one thing, but instead several individual mechanical components inside your body. These components must be located, developed, and taught to work with the other components harmoniously. The voice is like playing an instrument in the dark...without any hands. Every sound you make with your voice is connected to a feeling, or rather a series of feelings inside your body. The goal with this system of voice training is to develop a deep connection with your instrument....your body...your voice.

FUNDAMENTALS

The Four Parts of the Voice:

The *four parts of the voice* form a perfect democracy. They consist of:

1. *The Inner Ear:* The subjects of The Inner Ear relate to musicianship (i.e. pitch, note choice, rhythm, etc.) and instrument specific recognition (i.e. tone, inflection, volume, attitude, etc.) Although a singer's musicianship is greatly enhanced by this program due to the methodology of its teaching, the primary focus of the first four volumes of this system is instrument specific recognition via mechanics and technique training. So, always remember, the first part of the voice is "The Inner Ear."

2. *The Throat:* Think of the throat as a big circle including the mouth, tongue, larynx (Adam's Apple) and all of the muscles and cartilages from the face down to the shoulders. The vocal cords are the beginning source of all actual sound from the voice. They are housed in the larynx and are surrounded by several muscles that can either greatly enhance their performance or greatly hinder it. This is such an important subject to grasp for both proper vocal hygiene and good tone production.

3. *Support System:* All of that which is connected with the control of breath, basically your entire torso, is what makes up your "support system." Breath is the fuel for tone production. Without fully controlled support in singing, interesting and varied tone production is severely restricted. It is also important to recognize that several of the vocal health problems that localize in the throat can be cured by proper breath support.

4. *Resonance:* The sympathetic vibrations of your entire body, intensifying the tiny vibrations started in the throat by the vocal cords, is the definition of resonance. Enough emphasis cannot be placed on how small the initial tone produced by the vocal cords is. Often called vocal folds these tiny mucosa-lined ligaments (the vocal folds actually consist of five layers of tissue with muscle tissue in the center) vibrate much like the strings of an acoustic instrument, at varying speeds, to produce the initial pitch and tone of the instrument (There are several studies as to the specific functions of the vocal cords, which we'll talk more about later, but for now just think of them as the strings to your instrument). The rest is left up to articulation in the mouth and resonance in the head and body. Just as with any great acoustic instrument resonance in voice production plays such an important role in the overall tonal characteristics that its cultivation cannot be over-stressed.

THE STEREO ANALOGY
OF THE FOUR PARTS OF THE VOICE

I like to compare the four parts of the voice to a stereo system. Through specific training your ear becomes the recorded material e.g. your CD collection.

Your throat, being the first medium of sound production, can be compared to the CD player. Your support system (breath) fuels the tone, and can be compared to the amplifier. And your body is the source of resonance and tone projection, and can therefore be compared to a speaker system.

BEFORE WE GET STARTED
For the Supposedly Tone Deaf

If you are already someone with a pretty good musical ear then please move on to "Getting Started." If, on the other hand, you are among the ranks of the "supposedly tone deaf," here's what you need to do before you get started with the program. You need to find, buy, or borrow a keyboard of just about any kind. An inexpensive kid's keyboard will work just fine, but of course a higher quality unit might make things even easier.

Right out of your speaking voice, I would like for you to count from one to ten. With each number sustain the vowel just a little longer (i.e. one, two..uuu, three...eeee, etc,) You are speaking these numbers on a pitch (a specific vibrating frequency, i.e., a C, C#, D, etc.). It is important here that you identify the pitch you are speaking on with a pitch on the keyboard. Try staying on the same pitch for now if you can. You may need someone to help you identify the pitch at first, but once you know the general area of your speaking voice, you should be able to match it to a note on the keyboard by yourself after a little while. Once you can do this, pick a vowel (a, e, i, o or u) and really hear yourself matching the pitch of that vowel with the pitch you are playing on the keyboard. Now begin descending one note at a time on the keyboard and following with your voice. After a few notes come back up to where you started and this time, ascend past it by a few notes. Repeat this exercise several times growing a little further each time. This may take you several days (or longer) until this becomes easy and consistent for you, but with patience it will pay off greatly. After this exercise is under your control, begin to move by two notes at a time (i.e. white note to white note with a black note in between) along with the keyboard. Once your ear can easily follow the keyboard around, you are ready to move on with the program. There will be more ear training later on, but this should be enough to get you started. I don't really believe in a "tone deaf" ear, just an uneducated and possibly, tired ear. So, be patient and gentle and your ear will wake up and grow right along with the rest of your voice.

GETTING STARTED

We start with the throat as it is the first mechanical component of the voice and the initial source of our tone. It is also the only part of the voice which physically suffers when we abuse it. You must master the art of a tension free throat to sing healthily and to realize the voice's maximum potential. A singer must first learn to completely relax the constrictor muscles in the throat. These are the muscles used to lower the epiglottis in swallowing so that food and water do not pass down the trachea, but instead down the esophagus. These muscles are so often

ex. 1a

ex. 1b

ex. 1c

ex. 1d1

used that their natural reaction is to over-react in the singing process. Most singers start out by trying to sing like a balloon. When we squeeze air out of a ballon, the tip vibrates creating a tone. The harder you squeeze the air and the closer you pinch the end of the balloon together, the higher the pitch of the tone. Yes, pitch and tone mean different things. Pitch is what note you play and tone is how it sounds. Our throat isn't a balloon. We need to keep our throat open so that the vocal cords can vibrate freely. By constricting the throat and using the additional air needed to create a higher pitch (the higher the pitch, the faster the vibration necessary by the vocal cords), we not only severely kill our tone, but we run the risk of over-pressurizing our vocal cords, which can result in serious vocal health complications. The tone dies because the throat is ultimately the tone passage and by constricting, we make that passage smaller which results in a skinnier overall tone. So be healthy and sound good, relax your throat. See diagrams 1a. and 1b on page 16.

THE SEVEN POINTS OF RELAXATION

If you look at diagram # 1b, you will see how all of the muscles in your face, neck and throat are tightly intertwined. The purpose of the *Seven Points of Relaxation*, is to use your hands to loosen and relax these muscles from the "outside," so that the feeling of relaxation will grow to a deeper level "inside" your throat.

1. *Down the Face (see ex. 1a):* Gently rub down the face with finger tips.

2. *Jaw Hinge (see ex. 1b):* Massage deeply at the jaw hinge in front of the ears, at the pressure point of the jaw directly under the earlobes, and warble (shake fairly vigorously) the cheeks.

3. *Stretch Jaw (see ex. 1c):* Using your index fingers and your thumbs, gently stretch the jaw downward and then back upwards to close your mouth. Do this a few times until you feel no resistance from the jaw hinge.

4. *Root of Tongue (see ex. 1d1, 1d2, 1d3):* Use these examples to align your fingers properly, then place your finger tips on the bottom of your chin. Move them back towards the throat until they slide up to the soft, spongy muscle that is the root of your tongue. Now swallow. The root of the tongue should stiffen up and push your finger tips down. If this happens, you are in the right place. Now with a piston action, alternating up and down with your fingers, massage this area. Singers with long fingernails might try wearing gloves of some kind to avoid any unnecessary discomfort. The goal is to get this area com-

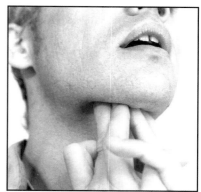

ex. 1d2

pletely loose and relaxed. Practice talking on different pitches while massaging this area. Try to keep the root of your tongue completely soft and relaxed while you're talking on these different pitches. This is a key area to eliminate constriction in the throat during phonation (producing voice).

5. *Horizontal Larynx (see ex. 1e):* With your palms facing out, place your finger tips on the outside of the ligaments surrounding your larynx. If this is uncomfortable, try using the fingertips and thumb of one hand to move the larynx. Be careful to still keep your fingers on the outside of the ligaments surrounding the larynx. Never move the larynx by touching it directly. Keep your finger tips low so that you are not pushing on the glands under your jaw. Gently move your larynx side to side, pushing with one group of fingers, then the other. If you are feeling or hearing any clicking in the throat, this is do to built-in tension in the ligaments surrounding the larynx. Be gentle, this clicking should go away after your throat learns to relax. Don't push your larynx very far to either side, a little horizontal movement is all we need here. This will not only help loosen and relax this area, but will also stimulate some nice circulation as well.

ex. 1d3

6. *Back of Head and Neck (see ex. 1f):* Imitating lobster claws with your fingers and thumbs massage the back of your head and neck. There is a nice pressure point at the base of the skull that should eliminate a lot of tension in your neck.

7. *Shoulders (see ex. 1g):* Also using the lobster claw hands, massage the muscles in your shoulders.

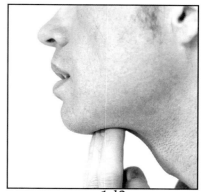

ex. 1e

DROOL EXERCISE

This is a throat relaxation and warm up exercise. The tangible result of this exercise is to be so relaxed in the throat so that you're stimulating the salivatory glands. This level of relaxation helps insure that the constrictor muscles in the throat will not interfere with comfortable and healthy singing (See diagram 1a to see how muscles connect). Really capture this feeling and learn to maintain it throughout your singing no matter how dynamic.

Listen now to example on **Volume One** recording.

If in doubt about the volume of this exercise, you're too loud. The *Drool Exercise* consists of the vowels "a," "e," "i," "o," and "u," preceded by the consonant "h" for a nice gentle entry into the note. Use the first five notes of the major scale in a very comfortable location

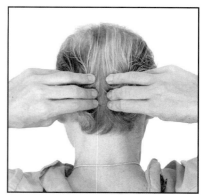

ex. 1f

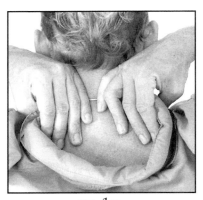

ex. 1g

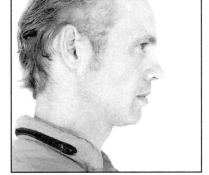

ex. 2a1 - correct

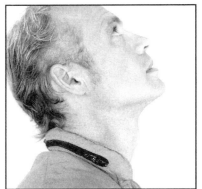

ex. 2a2 - incorrect

in your singing range (i.e. the lower middle) and repeat those exact notes repeating each vowel about five times. Men's starting note should be somewhere around a B flat to C (an octave below Middle C) Women's starting note should be somewhere around F to G (just below Middle C). If, in either case, these starting notes (for this or any other exercise in this program) don't work for you, experiment until you find a more comfortable place in your singing range. Keep your mouth very small and completely limp during this exercise. In this system, we are looking for *minimal mouth movement.* Excessive mouth movement invariably translates into unnecessary tension reaching well down into the throat. If it sounds like you're mumbling a little just now, don't worry about it, we'll talk about different mouth shapings and articulation techniques later on. On every other vowel ("he" and "ho") incorporate the *seven points of relaxation,* and really feel yourself going limp in this area. It is while adding these *points of relaxation* that you will most likely begin to feel "the drool" kick in. Once you can easily tap into this feeling, you will be able to do so throughout your singing session.

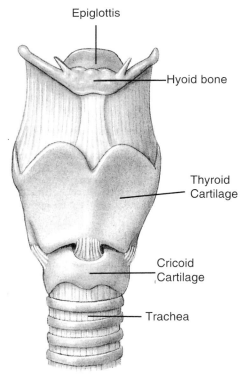

Diagram 1a

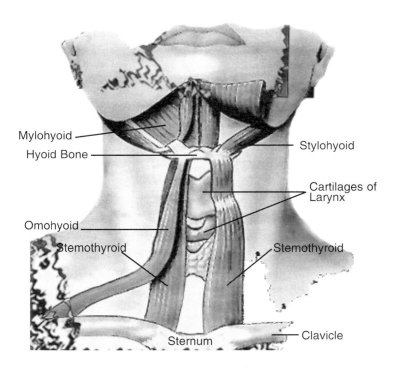

Diagram 1b

Using Ha (sounds like "hey") about 5 times
ha – ha – ha – ha – ha – ha – ha – ha – ha
Over the first 5 notes of the major scale:
do – re – mi – fa – sol – fa – mi – re – do

Then use "He" (sounds like "he/she") x about 7-10 times adding the 7 points of relaxation.
Then, on the same notes sing, "Hi" (sounds like "high") about 5 times
Then, using "Ho" (like Santa, only much quieter) about 7-10 times, adding the 7 points of relaxation.
And finally, using "Hu" (sounds like "who") about 5 times.

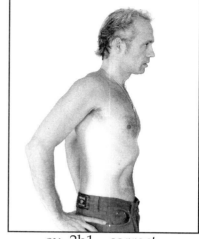

ex. 2b1 - correct

POSTURE

80% of posture relates directly to the support system. The better your singing posture, the better your breath control will be. This is because we are trying to create a support system that works more from reflexes than from direct manipulation of the abdominal muscles and diaphragm. The key to posture is alignment. If you align your body properly your support system will be free to work on this new high level necessary in singing. The other 20% of posture is related to the throat (open tone passage), and resonance (different cabinet sizes and shapes effect vibration characteristics).

The Three Focal Points of Posture:
(see three step wall method for basic body posture, page 18)

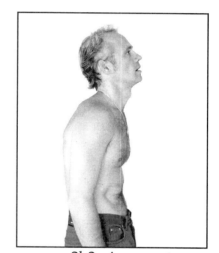

ex. 2b2 - incorrect

1. *Head (see ex. 2a1, 2a2):* Tilt slightly down at a 45° to set up what we refer to as "the basic shape of the throat." This helps prevent stretching and tightening of t he muscles in the throat, freeing the overall infrastructure of the larynx.

2. *Hips (see ex. 2b1, 2b2):* Pulled under in a pelvic tilt to straighten back as much as possible. This is done to free up the lower and middle abdominal muscles. These are constricting/anti-constricting muscles and must be free to move out on the inhale and, in on the exhale. Do not arch the back. Arching the back tightens these muscles and severely restricts their freedom.

3. *Rib Cage (see ex. 2c1, 2c2):* An "open rib cage technique" is used in *The Art of Body Singing*. If you study the mechanics of breathing in a book on anatomy, you will generally find a description of what's called "costal breathing." This basically means that the rib cage expands during inhalation and collapses during exhalation. This is fine for everyday use, but in singing, far more control and endurance are required than can be achieved by "costal breathing." An "open rib cage technique" is maintained by using the external intercostal muscles

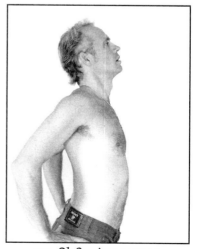

ex. 2b3 - incorrect

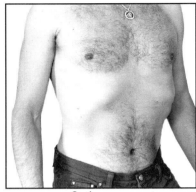

ex. 2c1 - correct

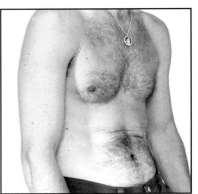

ex. 2c2 - incorrect

(the outside group of muscles located in between the ribs) to raise the ribs and expand the chest (see diagram #2 on page 20). If the "open rib cage technique" is maintained during singing, then you are no longer relying on the the rib muscles for exhalation, but instead upon the much more powerful and controllable diaphragm and abdominal muscles below your lungs.

It must be noted here that many systems teach diaphragmatic breathing in a collapsed chest posture. It is my belief that for less demanding singing this can certainly be adequate. However, it is also my belief that for more demanding singing, this is highly inadequate. The problem is that you will begin to push and shove with your diaphragm and abdominal muscles. This is often the cause behind many vocal health problems, a result of over-pressurizing the vocal cords. Pushing with the support system also tends to produce a very harsh and undesirable sounding tone. Even if you are trying to achieve a very grindy, aggressive tone, pushing is not how you'll achieve it. The big advantage to the "open rib cage technique" is freedom. This technique frees up the diaphragm and upper abdominal muscles so that they may be used more upon reflexes than by conscious manipulation. That benefit alone can dramatically influence a more relaxed delivery in a singer. So, spend some time developing this posture. What feels awkward at first will soon become so natural that anything less will be obviously inferior.

Three Step Wall Method for Attaining Posture:

Stance 1

1. *Sitting against the wall (see ex 3a).* Stand with your back against the wall, with your shoulders down and relaxed, and your hips in a pelvic tilt position (tilt your pelvis forward as if you are trying to relocate your tailbone directly under your belly button, while keeping your shoulders back), keeping your knees as bent as

necessary to feel your the wall (almost a sit-head down to a 45°. feet under your body touching the wall. slightly bent to main-

2. *Step out over front* away from the wall inant foot (if you're probably your right percent of your weight Think of a line run-

entire back touching ting position). Tilt Slowly walk your until your heels are Keep your knees tain a straight back.

foot (see ex. 3b). Step over your front dom-right handed that's foot) placing seventy over that front foot. ning under the toe of

ex. 3a

ex. 3b

ex. 3c

your back foot. The heel of your front foot should now be on that same line (in other words, don't step out too deep). Your feet should be about shoulder width apart. Come up on the ball of the back foot leaving thirty percent of your weight over that foot. In fact, think of most of your weight being placed on the balls of both of your feet. Be sure not to lose any of the alignment achieved in step 1. When necessary you should be able to shift weight easily from front to back feet without losing your body alignment. This comes in very handy when singing and playing an instrument simultaneously.

ex. 4a

3. *Lift into open rib cage position (see ex. 3c, also diagram 2).* Imagine a cable attached to your chest. As you take a deep breath way down into your body, while opening your rib cage with your intercostal muscles (not your back muscles), that cable is going to lift your torso up about an inch and keep it there. In other words, if you were wearing a long robe that touched the floor this step in posture would lift that robe off the floor by about one to one and one half inches, and keep it raised from breath to breath. Be careful to acknowledge that this is the torso lifting the robe and not the shoulders. Keep your shoulders down and relaxed. Do not allow your chest to collapse during singing or between breaths. If you do collapse, you will not realize the full range motion of the support system, and this will severely limit the endurance and control of your breath in singing. After some practice, you should be able to lift your chest and expand your upper rib cage without the aid of taking a breath. When you can do this, you will have truly discovered the independence of the intercostal muscles.

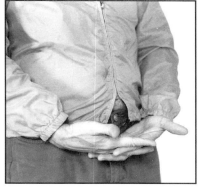

ex. 4b

Practice these steps until you can easily just step into posture from a standing position. Really teaching your body to maintain these alignments will take some weeks of practice. It will feel rather wooden at first, but I assure you that it will become very natural and supple with time.

THE KICK START TECHNIQUE

This technique is to be used with the following exercise:

1. *Thumbs on navel as measuring guide (see ex. 4A).* Lace fingers together with palms facing body. Place thumbs on naval (as a measuring guide) and cup lower edge of hands down under your belt line to the lower abdominal muscles. At this point palms should be facing upward.

2. *Cupped hands on lower abs (see ex. 4b).* Gently lift (never push) lower abdominals while practicing the *The Way Down Exercise.* This is to help locate and stimulate these lower deeper muscles.

THE WAY DOWN EXERCISE

There are a few objectives with this exercise. The title, *The Way Down Exercise*, means that you are singing *way down* in your range (very low notes), and that you are focusing *way down* in your support system (the lower abdominal muscles). The other objective with this exercise is to focus on maintaining your high chest and open rib cage position.

Some systems only develop the upper abdominal muscles and the diaphragm for breath support. Be aware that the closer the muscles are to the lungs, the higher the possibility of forcing air, which inevitably leads to oversinging and strain. This is invariably the case when singing the lower range. This is due to the fact that pitch is created by the speed at which the vocal cords vibrate. The higher the pitch, the faster the speed of vibration. The lower the pitch, the slower the speed of vibration. These vibrations are directly affected by the amount of air used during phonation (creating sound with voice). Therefore, working out in your lower range is a great place to get acquainted with the lower support system. These lower abdominals are farther away from the lungs and make for wonderful fine tuning support system muscles. Also, don't forget that even though you're stimulating these lower abs with the *kick start technique,* you don't want to develop any habits of squeezing or over firming anywhere in your support system. You are not looking for rock hard firmness, but instead a more supple firmness that can shift support from lower to upper abdominals and diaphragm very quickly and easily.

Pay close attention to how this exercise sounds on the Volume One recording. Remember not to gargle the tone as you go lower in your range,

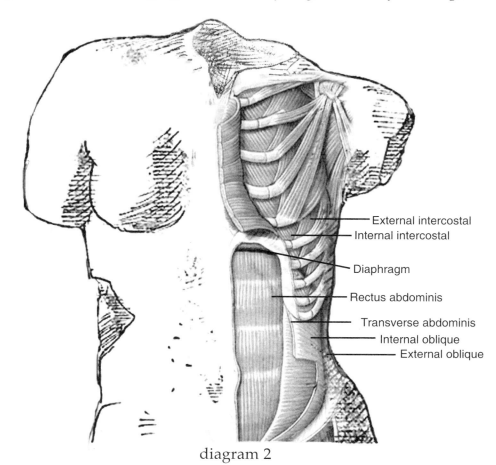

External intercostal
Internal intercostal

Diaphragm

Rectus abdominis

Transverse abdominis
Internal oblique
External oblique

diagram 2

but instead to *release* the tone. As you get lower and lower (all the way down to the *no note district*), the size of the tone should diminish until it is completely inaudible. This is to help you teach yourself not to let the tone be manipulated by the constricting muscles in the throat. In many ways this exercise should be an extension of the *Drool Exercise*, the end result being a warmed up and relaxed throat.

Listen now to example on **Volume One** recording.

Standing in your new, great singing posture, watch yourself in a mirror as you practice the exercise (a mirror will save you a lot of time in really learning to sing in posture). Your objective is to sing the exercise in its entirety without allowing your posture to deteriorate. The first thing to watch for is your ribs collapsing and your chest sinking. It is difficult at first to differentiate the intercostal muscles used to maintain the open rib cage position from the air in the lungs. It is very tempting at first to resort back to the much easier costal breathing (meaning that the rib cage and chest expand with inhalation and collapse with exhalation). It takes some practice, but it is important that you teach yourself to maintain the big open posture. Don't worry if the lower ribs shrink with exhalation. It is the upper ribs and chest that concern us most. Also, watch in the mirror that your head does not start rising up and that you do not begin arching your back.

The *Way Down Exercise* is done on repeated pitches using the musical consonant "m" with five vowels creating a *continuous energy* non-breaking tone. That means you hum the "m" between the vowels "e" (see), "a" (rhymes with say),"i" (try), "o" (go) and "u" (true) while singing the same pitch five times on one breath without stopping the tone.

Me, Ma, Mi, Mo, Mu

Use nice, relaxed, slightly airy (without pushing) medium-sized tone. Start in your lower middle range (men start around D below Middle C and women start around G below Middle C). Sing through all of the vowels sustaining the last one ("u") until you are nearly out of breath. Then move the vowel down one half step. Stop singing, but maintain the big open posture. Take a huge breath, through your nose and down into your lower abdominals, then start the series over on the new lower note. This is known as "moving the exercise." If you don't have an instrument handy, just start in a comfortable place in your range. Ultimately, you need to learn to do these exercises completely out of your head anyway. So, once you've memorized the exercise, start practicing without a reference note from an instrument. This is necessary to teach you self-sufficiency, as ultimately the voice is a free-standing instrument.

SPEAKING THE MELODY

It is very important that a singer understands the connection between singing and speaking. Any melody that can be sung can also be spoken. The biggest departure from speaking to singing is in the rhythm. With singing, we begin to sustain the vowels that in speaking, we cut short. Though they are gen-

THE ART OF BODY SINGING by BRECK ALAN

erally located in a narrow part of the vocal range, if you listen closely to most speaking voices you will hear plenty of melodies. This is, in fact, the premise to most contemporary systems of voice "if you can speak, you can sing." While there is certainly a lot of truth in that statement, it is my view that singing and speaking are first cousins, not twins. The singers that wish to elevate themselves to *high-level singing* must assemble a far superior instrument (voice) to the singer satisfied with the thin "speak-singing" voice so prevalent in today's contemporary music.

That said, the advantages to first learning this exercise of *Speaking the Melody* must not be overlooked. Those advantages include comfort, coordination, and naturalization. Singing is "connecting the dots" and is truly a democracy of its four components (1. Inner Ear, 2. Throat, 3. Support System, 4. Resonance). The easiest way to achieve this coordination is by concentrating largely on comfort. Keep things light at this stage in your development. In fact, I call this period of a singers growth *The Ease*, because I want their singing to have a nice easy quality to it. It is far too common in contemporary singing systems to have singers shouting at the beginning of their development. These "shouting" techniques are usually taught in the guise of "support system development" and "voice opening techniques." I disagree with this approach. I feel it can only teach singers the bad habits of pushing and straining from the beginning of their study. It is far more constructive to teach singers comfort, control and coordination from the get-go. This will make graduating into more ambitious singing a realistic transition.

It is often during *the ease* period that I will suggest a singer spend some time with some old jazz standard ballads. These tunes are conducive to a lighter touch. Ballads in general are great for developing breath support and, in my opinion, the older jazz is a sophisticated, yet straight forward style of music that can do nothing but wonderful things for a singer's ear. I must certainly pay tribute to a former teacher of mine, Steve Heck, for enlightening me to the virtue of singing Jazz Standards.

Also, by *Speaking the Melody* you can listen at this very formative time for that certain *singy* quality singers tend to get. This is a good time to think about being very dry and style-less in your singing. This will make way for a very natural, personal and honest delivery with your music. If you are practicing this technique with music other than your own, really try to hear your own speaking voice come through. It is my view that imitation in vocal technique training can be more of a hindrance than a help, especially at the beginning. For one, it takes a singer a long time to accurately register what they're hearing when they produce sound with their voice. Anyone who's recorded themselves and listened back to the results can attest to this reality. This is due to the vibrations occurring inside your head during phonation in conjunction with the sound exiting your mouth. It's a strange mixture. Therefore, if you are hearing something from the receiving end, and trying to reproduce it from the giving end, your challenge is obvious.

Some singers, though with some diligence, tend to master the art of imitating a few of their heroes. The problem with this approach is that their personal interpretation skills are limited to something akin to muscle memory singing. Regardless of the mood of the piece, their techniques are limited to what they learned through imitation and always sound the same. So do yourself a favor, and start naturalizing your voice through this wonderful exercise of *Speaking the Melody.*

Listen now to example on **Volume One** recording.

After warming up with the exercises you know so far, choose one or two songs with which you are already fairly familiar. If you can't think of one, try a children's song or perhaps a Christmas song that you already know and enjoy. Sing through a section of the song (a verse or chorus, etc...) a few times in a very comfortable voice. Begin hearing yourself curtail the lengths of the vowels in the song more and more until you are literally *Speaking the Melody.* If, at any point, you're having difficulty, lower the melody in pitch. It's important to understand the exercise, and then gradually make the difficulty level higher.

THE 3 AIR RATIOS

Air passing through the vocal cords, causing them to vibrate produces the initial pitch and tone for voice production. We then turn those initial vibrations into bigger tones with "resonance" from our body (discussed at length later in the program). Therefore, we can conclude that resonance plus air equals tone. Knowing this allows us to understand that there is always air under the tone. *The 3 Air Ratios* helps us to identify the air on top of the tone (sometimes referred to as "free air.")

1. Number One Ratio or Fully Supported Tone (see diagram # 3): On this *ratio* the air is completely underneath the tone. This is the most efficient tone you will produce. This is the tone heard from most healthy speaking voices, because it is the most projecting tone for the least amount of energy used. As an advanced singer, this is the biggest (meaning loudest and most resonant) tone you will ever produce, because all of the air used is being

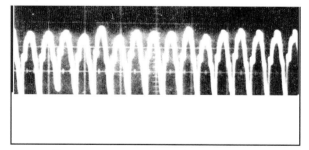

Tone

Support
Air

Diagram 3 - Number 1 Ratio

turned into resonance. You will also find that as you sing higher and higher in your range this will be the hardest *ratio* to maintain. This difficulty is due to unnecessary muscle constriction in the throat and very often from excess pushing from the support system, both contributing to an excessive level of *throat pressure* (covered later under this subject). So, for now, stay with *the ease* and gain the coordination to take this *ratio* to the top of your singing range.

2. ***Number Two Ratio or Full Tone with Air (see diagram 4):*** This is still a sizable tone, but with a very audible bite taken out of it. Using the same amount of energy used for a *number one ratio*, this tone will be lighter and have a wet airy quality to it (see *buffer air* below). As you sing higher in your range this tone should be easier at first to execute than the *number one ratio* tone. This once again is due to the subject of *throat pressure* (covered later in this subject).

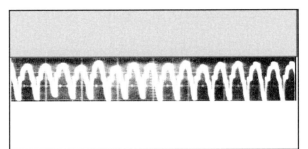

Buffer Air

Tone

Support Air

Diagram 4 - Number 2 Ratio

3. ***Number Three Ratio or Air Note (see diagram 5):*** Picture Marilyn Monroe singing "Happy Birthday, Mr. President." This is the lightest tone you will articulate and still be audible. This is a very wet and airy tone, but it is important to be aware of not creating excess air while singing the *number three ratio*. Remember, this is the same amount of energy used for the *number one ratio* , but with a significant *release* in the throat (see *buffer air* and *throat pressure* below).

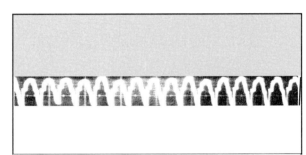

Buffer Air

Tone

Support Air

Diagram 5 – Number 3 Ratio

Listen now to example on **Volume One** recording...

1. Counting one through ten on the same pitch in a comfortable place in your range, switch from the *number one ratio* to the *number two ratio* and finally to the *number three ratio*. You should hear a very audible decrease in the volume of the more airy tones. Remember not to increase air as you're using *buffer air* here (see below). Start moving the pitch around in your range to fully experience the different *ratios*.

2. Now, begin sustaining the ratios. Starting in a comfortable place in your range using the word "hey," sustain the long "a" vowel, staying loyal to the ratio on which you began. Then, move on to the other two ratios and repeat. Once this is comfortable, move the pitch around in your range to fully experience sustaining the ratios. Remember to use your ear as your guide here. It is very common to start out on a *number one ratio* and slip to a *number two ratio*. Remember to *listen* for this and then *feel* the feeling involved in maintaining the ratio or adjusting back to the original ratio if you've slipped out. "Adjusting on the fly" is of primary importance in the performance world. Constantly recognizing that the ear is the first part of the voice will save you from the trap that many singers fall into of *auto-pilot singing*.

3. Now begin singing with the *three air ratios*: First, experiment with a short section of a song that you are familiar with (a verse or chorus, etc...). Start out singing the entire section on a *number three ratio* which should be the easiest of all (see *throat pressure*). Then, repeat the same section on a *number two ratio*, then finally a *number one ratio*. If the song is a little high in your range, you might experience some trouble with the *number one ratio* (see *throat pressure*). So, for now, sing the song lower in your range. Once this becomes comfortable, start practicing the ratios by staying loyal to one at a time for entire songs. This is not about interpretation just yet, this is about technique. The way to really learn a technique is by exaggeration. So, have fun with this.

TOOL SONGS

Now's a good time to pick out a couple of songs from your collection over which to practice your techniques. Keep it down to two or three songs for now. Sing these songs either along with a recording or A Capella. If you can play an instrument while singing, do so after you've had a good vocal workout. This way you can fully concentrate on the task at hand. Structuring a good singing session will be discussed later in this program.

THROAT PRESSURE

Throat pressure in singing is a very tricky subject. Especially since one of the first things we learn in proper vocalization is how to relax the constrictor muscles in our throat, so as not to over-pressurize our vocal cords. This makes the term *throat pressure* sound a bit contradictory.

Air passes through the trachea (windpipe) during the breathing process. During phonation, air stimulates the vocal cords (which are housed in the trachea inside the

larynx) causing them to vibrate, creating the initial pitch and tone. (See diagrams 6, 7, & 8). Because this miracle of voice production is so automatic to most humans, the initiation of the vocal cords is basically an involuntary one. Muscles and a pair of pivoting cartilages (the arytenoid cartilages) in the larynx are employed (largely by the nervous system) to bring the cords to their close, yet slightly apart position for proper vibration (see diagram 7 and 8). When the cords are properly aligned during phonation, one should experience (when concentrating) a mild sensation inside the throat. There should be absolutely no discomfort.

This sensation should be thought of as *conversation level throat pressure*. The reason for the term *throat pressure,* is that when the vocal cords come together there is a slight pressure created between the cords and the air in the lungs. It is this slight pressure that creates the initial vibration in the cords that can then be amplified by additional vibration throughout the body ("resonance" will be covered at length later in this program). This slight *conversation level throat pressure* is both necessary and healthy. What's unhealthy is any additional *throat pressure* caused by constriction in the throat or pushing too much air *through the throat* from the support system. Therefore, you must learn to take the journey inward, inside the throat and *feel* for that perfect level of *throat pressure*. Not only will it mean everything to your vocal health to master this feeling, but also to your tone quality (more about that later).

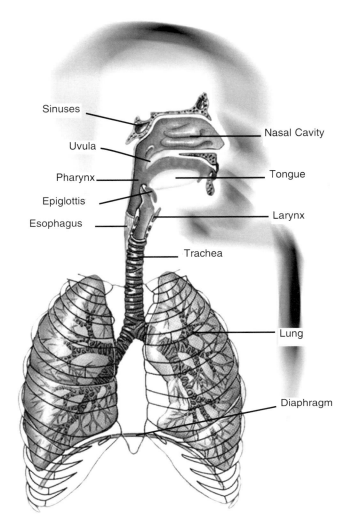

Sinuses

Nasal Cavity

Uvula

Pharynx

Tongue

Epiglottis

Esophagus

Larynx

Trachea

Lung

Diaphragm

Diagram 6

BUFFER AIR

I like to illustrate *buffer air* in relation to the *Three Air Ratios*. If there were a *ratio four*, it would be zero *throat pressure*, It would also be zero vibration of the cords and therefore zero tone. It would basically be air passing through the trachea and vocal cords without producing any vibration. Remember, without a slight pressure between the cords and the air in the lungs there can be no vibration of the cords. At *number three ratio*, the ords move closer together and we begin to pressurize a bit of air, resulting in cord vibration and the beginning of tone. At a *number two ratio,* the cords

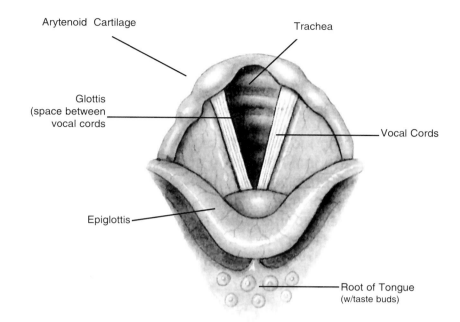

open position
Diagram 7

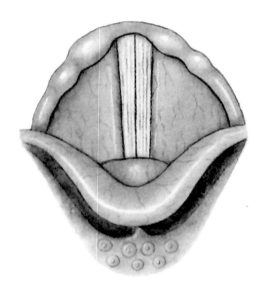

closed position
Diagram 8

move even closer together and we pressurize a bit more still, resulting in a very noticeable increase in tone color and volume using the same exact amount of energy and air. And finally, at a *number one ratio*, the cords come as close as they can for healthy singing, resulting in what's referred to as a "fully supported tone."

With over-pressurization, the cords begin to touch (somewhat violently), causing irritations leading to vocal disorders. There should be no audible air on top of the *number one ratio*. And, for the same amount of energy used for the airier *ratios,* this should be the loudest and fullest tone of all. As stated earlier, the higher in your range that you sing, the more likely you are to over-pressurize the *number one ratio*. This is because it requires more air for the vocal cords to vibrate at a faster speed to create the higher pitch. This makes maintaining *conversation level throat pressure* in the upper range difficult. It simply requires some methodical and patient practice, as well as some great techniques which we'll learn later on in the system. So for now, stay with *the ease* and just master the different techniques you've been learning thus far. We'll get to the tough stuff soon enough.

GUSHING

Listen to example on **Volume One** recording.

Gushing is a random release of air during phonation. It is usually a result of pushing with the support system. Check your posture and back off! We are currently observing a *No Black Sheep Rule* in our practice sessions. This implies that we are *listening* to ourselves and making corrections where they need to be made. If you maintain *buffer air*, *gushing* will not be possible.

THE TONGUE ROLL AND LIP ROLL

These two exercises are very popular in contemporary singing systems, and there is good reason for this. When done correctly, they are wonderful mechanics exercises. They help coordinate the *four parts of the voice* beautifully.

ex. 5a

The Tongue Roll is executed like a spanish "r." The tip of the tongue vibrates against the hard corner of the gum ridge, behind the top front teeth and the sharp rising arc of the hard pallet, while creating a tone with the vocal cords. If you are not getting a tone with the vibration of the tongue, you will be creating what some diction systems call an unvoiced consonant (a consonant produced without the aid of the vocal cords). In this instance, the consonant will be a "t" sound as in "time." Think more along the lines a vibrating "tr," as in "truck," or, for a softer entry into the exercise, try "dr" as in drive. At first, just practice short and gentle entries with this exercise. Once you get the hang of it move on to the extended exercises listed below.

"The Lip Roll" is executed by puckering your lips forward with your thumb and index finger placed in the dimple area of the cheeks, pushing slightly out and slightly up to create loose and relaxed lips (see ex 5a). Roll the lips (sometimes called "bubbles," "raspberries," "car revving," etc...), while creating a tone with the vocal cords. If you are vibrating your lips, but not initiating a tone, you are probably concentrating on the consonant "p" (you can produce "p" without creating tone from the vocal cords). Instead, concentrate on the consonant "b" with your entries into the Lip Roll, as this should help facilitate the tone.

Here are the rules for the mechanics of both the Tongue Roll and the Lip Roll. In both exercises, concentrate on how slow and relaxed you can make the vibration of the tongue or the lips. If either are vibrating in a fast, spasmodic sort

THE ART OF BODY SINGING by BRECK ALAN

of way, you are "over-singing." This means that you are singing *through your throat* instead of *behind your throat*. Something you will hear a lot in *The Art of Body Singing* is to sing *backwards into the body*. Ultimately, this means you are going *inside your body* where everything happens in singing, and you are coordinating the process from its source. Everything in singing is connected to the series of physical feelings that make sound from the voice possible. If you are "over-singing," you are basically "pushing" air out of your lungs *through your throat* and singing from the throat up. This can result in a very unhealthy voice and, ultimately, bad tone.

Concentrate on a *number one ratio* for both the Tongue Roll and the Lip Roll. One of the most tangible assets of these two exercises is that much of the *throat pressure* needed for phonation is transferred from the throat to the lips or tongue (depending, of course, on which exercise you are practicing). You will clearly feel this with one of the up-coming exercises (TR mm ah and LR mm ah exercises). This makes practicing with the *number one ratio* very safe and practical at this time. Remember, the ear is the first part of the voice. If you're hearing air on top of the tone with these exercises, your not in a *number one ratio*. If you're having difficulty executing these exercises on the *number one ratio* practice altering from a tone on that *ratio* into the Tongue Roll or the Lip Roll exercises. Most students have an easier time with one or the other of these exercises. Some students, no matter how hard they try, can only execute one of the two exercises. And a small percentage of students cannot execute either of the exercises. It has been my experience that with practice most students can achieve great results with both exercises. If one is more difficult than the other, do not give up on it. Even though they appear very similar just now, they are different enough exercises that the ideal is to possess both. Thoroughly examining your mechanical difficulties in singing, and then overcoming them, will teach you far more than the techniques that come to you without any struggle.

If you think back in the program you might notice that the Drool Exercise was done basically on a *number three ratio*, the *Way Down Exercise* was done basically on a *number two ratio*, and now the Tongue Roll and Lip Roll should be done on a *number one ratio*. This structure is designed to enhance your sensibilities and ear to the *mechanical switch* requirements necessary in producing the different *air ratios*. This is also partly do to the practical process of warming up. With *buffer air*, the lighter the *ratio* (i.e. *number three ratio* being lightest), the easier on the throat. This is due to throat pressure. So, regardless of one's ability, always start with the lightest and progress to the more difficult.

Listen now to example on **Volume One** recording.

Start with a sustained Tongue Roll. Using a mirror to monitor excellent posture and the second hand of a clock to monitor progress, sustain a nice easy *number one ratio* Tongue Roll for as long as possible. Then move one half step in either direction and explore this exercise throughout your range. Keep it nice and comfortable. It will be more comfortable to use the airier ratios for the higher part of your range. That's ok for starters, but keep teaching yourself what it *feels* and *sounds* like as you keep shaving off the air. When it gets too high or low, reverse direction and work on coordination. If you're having trouble sustaining this exercise, really work on your entries. After your entries begin to smooth out (for many this is only after several tries) begin to draw them out to a more sustained Tongue Roll.

Men start around a D and women start around a G below Middle C. If these starting notes aren't comfortable, experiment until you find what suits you. Sustain the Tongue Roll as long as possible, then move the note one half step up or down, just before your air supply is completely exhausted. Repeat the exercise on a new note.

Repeat the exact procedure listed above with Lip Roll exercise.

THE "TONGUE ROLL MM AH" EXERCISE

This is a coordination exercise designed to get you from the ideal set-up of the Tongue Roll (or Lip Roll) exercise, to the nicely contained world of a healthy hum, to the more precarious world of creating a tone.

Listen to example on **Volume One** recording.

Note that the first examples on the recording are done on a *number two ratio* for ease and then changed to a *number one ratio*. Even though we are attempting to do the Tongue Roll and Lip Roll exercises on a *number one ratio*, our first concern is always comfort.

Without stopping the flow of tone, energy, or air, move seamlessly from a comfortable Tongue Roll to a comfortable hum on an "m," to a comfortable tone on "ah" (as is "ball"). Remember the *no black sheep rule*, and listen not to allow any changes from one part of the exercise to the next (i.e. differences in volume, pitch, or *air ratios*). Once the exercise becomes comfortable, it should be executed on the *number one ratio*.

Men start around a D and women around a G below Middle C. Move the exercise just before breath is completely exhausted and repeat exercise on new note.

Sustain the final tone in the exercise as long as possible. *Listen* and *feel* what this tone sounds and feels like. It should still be a *number one ratio*, and it should feel comfortable and sound clear. If you are hearing any *throat rattle* or *throat distortion* (see following explanation) being added to the tone you are pushing, so back off.

Repeat the above procedure for the *Lip Roll Mm Ah* exercise.

THROAT RATTLE OR THROAT DISTORTION

Throat rattle or throat distortion are caused by singing *through the throat* and rattling the phlegm and mucous that is generally present to one degree or another in all of our throats. In *The Art of Body Singing*, our goal is to sing *behind the throat* or *over the throat* and never *through the throat*. This is a strange concept for many at first, because it seems to create a contradiction in anatomy. This is ultimately about singing with the perfect *throat pressure*, and letting the other elements of the voice (i.e. resonance, ratios, etc,) create the size, color and projection you are after. *Throat Rattle* is an obvious sign of over-pressurizing in the throat, via constriction or pushing. So, correct this problem while we're still working on *the ease* level of energy.

You must constantly remember that singing is *connecting the dots*. Only so much can be expected from the throat, or from the support system, or from resonance. Any over-reliance on these individual parts will result in an obvious imbalance. Therefore, the answer is always in the correct distribution of responsibility between the components of the voice. Think of it as a true democracy. The end result of the *four parts of the voice* working in harmony together is so much greater than that of the voice where the power is in an obvious imbalance.

TONGUE ROLL 1-5 EXERCISE
AND THE LIP ROLL 1-5 EXERCISE

This helps develop the *air spigot* in your support system for singing. The *air spigot* is the imagery I use for the control of the support system. Air requirements are different as pitches vary. Use your ear as your guide in this exercise. If you're getting louder as you ascend in pitch, you are *overcompensating* the *air spigot* with too much air. If you are getting quieter as you sing lower, you are *undercompensating* the *air spigot* with too little air. Also, pay close attention that you don't change your *air ratio* as you move the pitch. This happens most commonly while ascending in pitch. This relates back to the issue of *throat pressure*. Your job here is to relax your throat and not allow your support system to push (the better the posture, the less likelihood of pushing). This is about management. Don't race through the exercise. Loop each series of notes several times until you're comfortable enough to move on. If your tone is getting bright (as in a falsetto kind of tone) as you enter into your upper range, that is just fine for now. Just keep it light and relaxed. We will deal with the subjects of tone quality and resonance at great lengths in the subsequent volumes.

Listen now to the example on **Volume One** recording.

Using the first five notes of the major scale, move the exercises up and down to develop the coordination necessary in moving a tone.

These are the same notes we used for the Drool Exercise, only now sustain the last note for a short time and then move the note one half step in whatever direction you are moving. Men start around a B or C one octave below Middle C and women start around a G below Middle C. Begin by moving the exercise upward (ascending) until it becomes too difficult, then begin looping one series of 1-5 at a time until it feels comfortable to move on. Once you've passed your comfort level, begin moving the exercise back down towards your lower range.

TONGUE ROLLING AND LIP ROLLING
OVER MELODIES

Once you've reached a certain comfort level with these exercises, Tongue Rolling and Lip Rolling over melodies is a great way to find a real fluidity in practicing them. This exercise also makes for a great warm up to do in the car. I'm not a big fan of car singing. I've seen too many strained voices as a result, but with a little understanding, there are certain things which can be practiced in the car. Of course, it is never advisable to do anything which might distract your driving, so always use discretion.

Listen now to example on **Volume One** recording.

Start with a few comfortable melodies that you already know. If you can't think of one, try a children's song or Christmas carol. Basically practice the Tongue Roll and the Lip Roll over these melodies. Stay light. Once it feels comfortable, start shaving off the air and moving closer and closer to a *number one ratio* for the entire melody. Once you've gone through your earlier warm ups, this is something that you can be doing throughout the day. This is a great coordination development exercise. Have fun!

SINGING AN OCTAVE BELOW THE MELODY

It is very common for singers to sing poorly in their lower range. This is mostly do to a lack of training in singing in their lower range. Most singers are so attracted to the acrobatic upper middle and upper range, that the lower range is often ignored. This seems a shame since singing is ultimately acting, and the emotions portrayed in the lower range can be strikingly different from the emotions portrayed in the upper range. Therefore, full range singing generally translates into a full range emotional performance. So kill multiple birds with one stone. Sing your lower range for relaxation, for comfort and safety in car singing, and for full range singing practice.

Listen now to example on **Volume One** recording.

Once you've warmed up, put on a recording of a song with which you are already familiar. Now gently sing along with that song on the proper melody. Once the melody is firmly in your ear, begin singing the same melody exactly one octave lower. This should be in a very relaxed and released tone much like that of the *Way Down Exercise*. This should not only be relaxing for your throat, but should prove to be a great workout for your lower range as well as for your ear. This is both a great relaxation exercise and a safe solution to car singing.

SILENT SINGING

Silent Singing is of course just that, singing completely in your head without uttering a sound. Silent Singing is a great exercise for your ear and your body. The first goal is to be able to sing silently and really monitor that no tension is building in your throat or anywhere else in your body. So be completely limp. Next try adding some of the physical mechanics (i.e. posture, air ratios, etc.) that you are currently learning (we will be adding many more mechanics in subsequent volumes). This is a good way to practice *feeling* inside your body at any given time or place. Try Silent Singing first with a song you know well, then add it to your list of safe car singing techniques (of course, never losing sight of the concentration necessary for driving).

YOUR VOLUME ONE WORK OUT AND WARM UP ROUTINE

Singing is a physical proposition. Warm Up! As we stated earlier in the program it might be easier for you to compile all of the exercise examples from the Volume One recording onto one tape. Do this in the order in which they appear in the program. Use that compilation tape to really grasp all there is to grasp from each exercise, and to memorize each exercise. Then begin practicing your routine completely from memory.

At this point use what we've learned in Volume One in the following order.

1. Drool Exercise with the Seven Points of Relaxation (2 minutes)
2. Way Down Exercise (2 minutes)
3. Timed Sustained Tongue Roll Exercise (2 minutes)
4. Tongue Roll Mm Ahh Exercise (2 minutes)
5. Tongue Roll 1-5 Exercise (2 minutes)
6. Timed Sustained Lip Roll Exercise (2 minute)
7. Lip Roll Mm Ahh Exercise (2 minutes)
8. Lip Roll 1-5 Exercise (2 minutes)
9. Light to Medium Sustained Tones Practicing Three Air Ratios (2 minutes)
10. Gently Speaking the Melody on Number One Ratio (2 minutes)

So far, that's just a well-organized twenty minute workout routine.

Now, practice singing using your *tool songs*. Start out very gently on a *number two ratio,* and feel how good it feels to be warmed up. Gently make the transition to the *number one ratio* without changing your energy. The size of the tone will automatically grow with this transition. Once you've stayed loyal to the *number one ratio*, begin deliberately varying the *ratios*. Absorb the differences in size, color and physical demands of the *three air ratios*.

Now, sing any other material you might be working on for as long as you have time. If that's only ten minutes, then so be it. But if it's longer, great. Stay relaxed, keep checking in with the mirror, keep using your hands to massage the *seven points of relaxation* (as tension can creep in at any time) and keep *listening* to yourself. Have a lot of fun and join us for Volume Two of *The Art of Body Singing*.

Best Wishes,

Please visit bodysinging.com to purchase easy to follow routine CDs of the exercises contained in this book.

THE
ART
OF
BODY
SINGING

VOLUME II

INTRODUCTION

Welcome back to *The Art of Body Singing*. We will be using the vocabulary established in Volume One, so please be familiar with it. We are still working on coordination here, staying light and looking for *the ease* in our singing. Getting the big size and growl in our tone is so much easier once we've achieved *the ease*. Our motto in this volume should definitely be "see, hear and feel." *See* yourself by doing a lot of mirror work and correcting what needs correcting. *Hear* the specific characteristics in your tone and identify those characteristics with your new vocabulary of singer lingo (which is about to get larger). *Feel* yourself making adjustments as your tone is changing at your command.

Remember to always warmup with the exercises learned in Volume One before working on the material in this volume.

RESONANCE

As we stated in Volume One, *air plus resonance equals tone*. Think of the voice as a combination horn/string instrument. The combination of air as the driving force for the voice, and the *throat pressure* described in Volume One, make up the horn part of this instrument. The combination of the vocal cords beginning the pitch/tone, and the resonating of the body to re-enforce those initial vibrations, make up the string instrument side of the voice.

"Resonance" is vibration. In singing, "resonance" is the sympathetic vibrations of the body to the smaller vibrations that begin in the throat (by the vocal cords). By themselves, the vocal cords can produce only the tiniest amount of size and color. The result of listening to the vocal cords by themselves would be much the same as listening to a string from an instrument (guitar, violin, etc.) by itself. String instruments are highly dependent upon their size, shape, and material to produce their recognizable tone. In this system, we are entirely dependent upon resonance for the color and size of our tone.

There are systems of study that teach exotic vocal cord manipulations and stretches for voice development. Although I have a lot of respect for many of the teachers and originators of these unique techniques, I personally am leery of their true substance, and quite genuinely afraid of the healthfulness of such techniques. Of course, as we learned in Volume One, and will continue to learn more about in this and subsequent volumes, there are many moving components in the voice. Much of this movement occurs in the throat and mouth, dramatically effecting tonal characteristics of the voice. These movements change the shape of the area directly surrounding the larynx, the oral cavity, and the nasal passage (see diagram #9). When you change the shape of any primary component on a musical instrument, the characteristics of the tone will change. It is with these physical adjustments that you will learn to create tones varying from the softest and sweetest to the hardest and nastiest in a completely healthy manner. If you regard the vocal cords with the utmost care and respect, asking of them only what they were designed to do, they should in turn honor you with many good years of service. Instead of pushing the vocal cords beyond their natural limits, you should instead push yourself to better navigate an instrument that involves the entire body. Only then will you step past the frustration with oversinging, into the world of *Body Singing.*

In your body, bone is the greatest conduit for vibration, although one can not discount the other vibrating matter, such as ligaments, fatty tissue, muscle, etc. Many Opera singers are of the opinion that they sing (resonate) all the way down to their toes. For

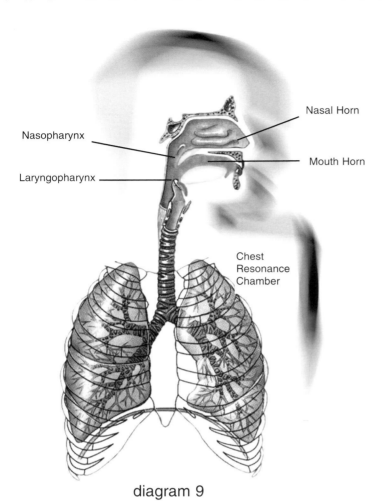

Nasal Horn

Nasopharynx

Mouth Horn

Laryngopharynx

Chest
Resonance
Chamber

diagram 9

those that truly understand "resonance" that is a good philosophy to live by. On the other hand, I have actually heard very accomplished teachers of voice state, "that as long as you're relaxed and you're support system is working properly, resonance will fall together. It's kind of like the icing on the cake." I'm afraid, I must disagree. In my opinion, "resonance" is the cake.

THE THREE RESONANCE CHAMBERS

In *The Art of Body Singing*, we break resonance down into *The Three Resonance Chambers*. These chambers are *The Chest Resonance Chamber*, *The Mouth Horn*, and *The Nasal Horn*. Each resonance chamber has a very distinct tonal quality. We must learn to identify each one individually, then we can begin to blend them together. First think of *The Three Resonance Chambers* as tone controls. The *chest resonance chamber* is your bass control, the *mouth horn* is your midrange control, and the *nasal horn* is your treble control.

Chest Resonance is produced from the larynx down. If you place your hand on your throat during phonation, you will feel quite a lot of vibration there. Now try placing your hand on your chest while speaking. You should feel some vibration happening there also. We will soon learn to "place" our resonance deeply into our *chest resonance chamber* for a fat bottom end to our tone. Do not confuse this with what is traditionally taught in many systems of singing as "head and chest voice." Head voice is traditionally defined as singing in your "upper register," and chest voice is traditionally defined as singing in your "lower register." This translates to what's called "multi register singing." That is not our pursuit in *The Art of Body Singing*. We are pursuing something far more natural sounding titled "one register singing," that we'll explore in much detail very soon.

Mouth Horn Resonance is produced from the larynx upward passing through what I like to think of as the *tone passage*, then resonating and exiting primarily in the mouth (oral cavity), most directly upon the soft palate. More technically the *tone passage* is called the "pharynx." (See Diagram #9) It is broken down into the "laryngopharynx" and the "nasopharynx." With *mouth horn resonance* we are, of course, concentrating on the laryngopharynx. The *mouth horn resonance chamber* helps provide the midrange to our tone. In a healthy speaking voice you hear it accompanied by the other resonance chambers to provide a rich balanced tone. The higher the pitch, the more recognizable the *mouth horn* becomes. When disconnected from the other *resonance chambers,* this tone becomes the bright, thin tone often associated with "falsetto." This is common among singers that are still suffering from the notorious "vocal break." That is the dramatic change in tone (the tone becomes very small and bright) that happens when entering the upper middle area of your singing range. This affliction can be reliably overcome once a solid understanding and aptitude of "resonance placement" and "one register singing" has been achieved. Once "one register singing" has been achieved, you can then use the *mouth horn resonance* as a color in any way you like. However, it will then be a choice as opposed to a condition.

Nasal Horn Resonance is produced by resonating primarily in the nasal cavities located in the nasal passage (placing resonance through the "nasopharynx"). By itself it is a very thin, buzzy, edgy, harsh tone. When compared with the other *resonance chambers* on the same pitch, using the same level of energy, this tone will sound much louder. This is one of the first principles in "projection" (a great word in singing, meaning "to fly through the air"). This is a solid principle in sound acoustics, "the brighter the tone, the more directional it is." This is why it is difficult for those without well trained ears to distinguish bass guitar tones. The easiest explanation would be because bass tones are very low in pitch and therefore very non-directional. And yet hearing a melody on a baritone saxophone, playing the same pitches as a bass guitar, is fairly easy for even the least trained ears in the room. This is because the baritone saxophone is a more directional and therefore a more projecting tone. It is important here to understand a little bit about a subject called "overtones," sometimes referred to as "harmonics" in music. When you hear a sound produced by virtually anything (but more apparent in a resonating musical instrument), what you are actually hearing is the fundamental tone produced upon attack (i.e. a hammer hitting the string on a piano). Then, you hear the series of overtones that effectively harmonize (any two notes played together constitute "harmony," while notes played separately are considered "melodic") with that original tone until its complete decay or premature ending (i.e. muting the note). Overtone values are different from one instrument to the next, due to the shape and material of the instrument. It is this difference that gives each instrument its own specific tone quality referred to as "timbre." And although the voice already has its own identifying timbre (unique and different with everyone), by highlighting different resonances in our body using our resonance placement skills, we are emphasizing different overtones, which will dramatically effect our *projection value.*

RESONANCE SHIFTING

To understand *Resonance Shifting* we must think vertically with our resonance. Do not confuse this with style. This is simply an exercise in exaggerating your resonance placement so that you can fluidly navigate the *three resonance chambers.*
Listen now to examples on **Volume Two** recording.

Start with the *chest resonance chamber*. In a comfortable place in your middle range, look in a mirror and lightly sing "ahh" on a *number one ratio*. Now, stop singing for a moment. Look at your throat in the mirror and try to yawn. If you can do this, you'll see your Adam's Apple "drop" a significant distance in your throat (this is sometimes

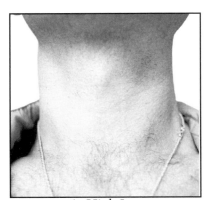
ex. 6a High Larynx

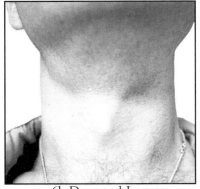
ex. 6b Dropped Larynx

referred to in singing as "yawning the Adam's Apple down" See ex. 6a and 6b). It is more difficult to see the Adam's Apple on a woman, but if you look closely you can see the movement downward in the throat or an arc downward where the chin meets the throat. (see ex. 8a & 8b). Once you are capable of "dropping your larynx," try keeping it down and repeat the "ahh" on the same easy pitch. This tone should sound very strange, dull and ultimately, not very loud. Strange, because by "dropping the larynx" we are changing the shape of the throat and therefore dramatically changing the shape of the tone; dull and quiet because the chest tone by itself is like having the midrange and treble controls turned completely off (which, of course, kills the projection value). Advanced singers are capable of adding the upper *resonance chambers* to their tone while maintaining the "dropped larynx position." We'll talk more about this fun subject later. For now, we are more interested in *tone isolation exercises* where we vertically shift from one *resonance chamber* to the other and distinctly hear and feel the dramatic difference between them.

Once you can successfully maintain a fully *isolated* tone in your chest by dropping the larynx, allow your larynx to rise in your throat and with it, the tone. This should sound natural in your comfortable middle range because this is the *mouth horn*, the most centered and natural of the *three resonance chambers* in the healthy speaking voice. As we stated earlier, the higher you are in your pitch with this resonance, the brighter it will become. Shift back and forth for awhile now between the *chest resonance chamber* and *mouth horn resonance* until this is very comfortable.

Now changing the vowel to a long "e" (as in "free"), begin directing the resonance into the *nasal horn*. Use the word "french" (sounds like "freench") to guide you into the *nasal horn*. There is an arc to the word "french" on the "e" vowel. It is this arc that should sound the most buzzy and edgy. This is the sound and feeling you want to capitalize on. Once you can clearly distinguish this arc, you should spend a lot of time trying to maintain the feeling necessary to sustain the *buzz* in the tone. This should certainly be the most projecting tone of the the *three resonance chambers*.

Once you are comfortable producing these tones by themselves (*tone isolation*), begin *resonance shifting* between the *three resonance chambers*. Use an "ahh" for the *chest resonance chamber* and *mouth horn*, and then switch over to a long "e" for the *nasal horn*. Once you are comfortable with *resonance shifting*, stay on a *number one ratio* for the duration of the exercise. This makes it much easier to discern the qualities of each individual *resonance chamber*.

The trick to getting deeper and deeper into each of the *three resonance chambers* lies in releasing any excess *throat pressure*, by relaxing the constrictor muscles or extrinsic larynx muscles in the throat (keep trying to kick into *the Drool*), and by eliminating any pushing from the support system. Also, *listen, listen, listen!* Remember, the first part of the voice is *the ear*. Then connect the ear to the internal series of feelings associated with producing sound from the voice. Think of this as a series of *switches* inside your body. Really identify those *switches* and learn how it feels to work them, at first individually. We will begin learning to put the switches together soon enough.

TONGUE POSITION

Controlling the tongue is an absolute must for a singer. Your tongue shape and position will dramatically effect your tone, articulation and overall ease of delivery. Your tongue shape will be slightly different with each vowel. Once your tongue coordination is under your control, it is my opinion that your ear should be the biggest guide to vowel inter-pretation. If one places rigid tongue and mouth shape requirements on a singer to achieve a specific vowel criterium, the end result is a very styl-ized sound. The goal with *The Art of Body Singing* is to reach a high level of technique and mechanical skills without over influencing the personal style of the artist.

Teach yourself to position your tongue flat on the floor of the mouth, with the tip of the tongue lightly touching the back of the teeth. You need to be able to groove your tongue in such a way that you can see the back of your throat (see ex. 7a and 7b of *grooved tongue position*). In fact, this is the result doctors get by suppressing your tongue with a tongue suppressor so that they may look completely down your throat for an examination. This is a good starting position for the tongue as it truly opens up what we call the *tone passage*. Of course, things will begin to move around once articulation begins, but once this reference has been established and you've learned to *hear and feel* the result of the *grooved tongue position*, you will become a believer.

It usually takes a few weeks to master the *grooved tongue position*. Of course, using the mirror a lot during practice can ensure that you are truly able to *see* what your tongue is doing while you're learning to *hear and feel* what it's doing.

TONGUE CONTROL EXERCISE
(In Conjunction with Dropped Larynx)

Both the *grooved tongue position* and the dropped larynx position are products of anti-constrictor muscle movement. The first thing you learned in this system was to relax the "constrictor muscles" in your throat. Now you are already working with the next step in *throat manage-ment*, "anti-constrictor muscle movement." Just think, if constriction is closing, then anti-constriction is opening. This is a very good thing! With "anti-constrictor muscle movement" it is important to observe some of the different feelings you might be experiencing in your throat. For one thing, even though you are still relaxing one group of muscles, you are activat-

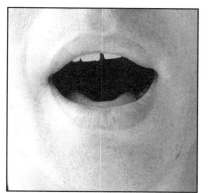

ex. 7a grooved tongue

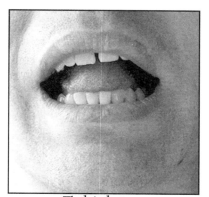

ex. 7b high tongue

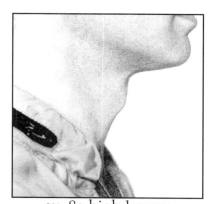

ex. 8a high larynx

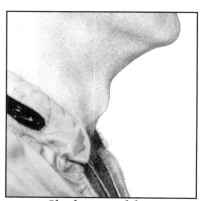

ex. 8b dropped larynx

ing another group. Therefore, as you groove your tongue and drop your larynx you should *see, hear and feel* a new sensation. There should now be a noticeable arc in the bottom of the chin where it meets the neck (See ex. 8a and 8b). There will now be varying degrees of stiffness here, but it will not be tension. Be sure and know the difference! The deeper you drop the larynx the more stiffness you will feel. This is just a product of the anti-constrictor muscles at work. At first, you may experience some fatigue in this area (not to be confused with vocal fatigue in the region of the vocal cords). This is normal, you are just activating and developing muscles that are not normally used to this degree. Also, be aware that although *grooving the tongue* and dropping the larynx are achieved from sympathetic muscle groups, there is certainly a large amount of independence that can be maintained between these two actions. This will become more and more important to you as you experiment with the tone differences achieved with varying levels of the dropped larynx. We will look at this subject more closely in the following exercise and then again on a larger scale later on in the program.

One of the most effective ways of learning to control the anti-constrictor muscles used in your tongue to achieve the *grooved tongue position* is through a conscious tongue relaxation exercise. Using the tip of your finger (wash your hands first) press down on the tip of your tongue. Your tongue (being the overactive muscle that it is) will push back. Keep pressing with your finger until you can consciously will your tongue to become limp and relaxed. Now move your finger to the middle of your tongue and repeat. Move further and further back until your finger is at the base of the tongue (if you should begin to gag cease exercise and resume shortly thereafter). Move your finger tip around to left and right from the center of your tongue and repeat exercise. Due to the extreme relaxation your tongue will be achieving, you will probably be drooling quite profusely. This is normal. Just by the conscious relaxation achieved by doing this exercise a few times, you should already have more control over your tongue. This is good, because now you must practice grooving your tongue while looking in a mirror over and over until you can easily do it. This is something you can practice several times throughout the day for just a few minutes each time. Maybe every time you go to the bathroom, you can spend a few extra minutes looking in the mirror and working on your *grooved tongue position.*

SUSTAINED TONE EXERCISE FOR GROOVED TONGUE IN CONJUNCTION WITH DROPPED LARYNX

Listen now to examples on **Volume Two** recording.

Do exercise using medium energy sustain tones, in your comfortable middle range, using the vowel "i" with an "h" in front of it (sounds like "high"). "I" is what's called a diphthong, meaning it is actually composed of two vowel sounds, "ah" (as in hot) and "e" (as in see). Therefore "i" equals "ahh-ee." More about that later, but for now "listen" to yourself and remember to stay on one part of the vowel at a time. In fact, for this exercise stay on the "ahh" part of the diphthong until the very end.

Hahhhhh-ee
The tongue must rise partially and change its shape to produce the "e" part of this diphthong. It is important that you *see, hear and feel* that when it happens.

Looking in a mirror, start off by simply experimenting with moving your tongue from a high position (see ex # 7b) to a lower grooved tongue position, (see ex #7a) sustaining a comfortable tone on the "ahh." There should be a very audible difference in the tone. Now take it one step further and drop your larynx as low as you can (see ex 6a and 6b). This should once again dramatically alter the sound of your tone. Don't try to "pull" the sound completely into your chest. You're not practicing a *tone isolation exercise* just now. You're just trying to alter an existing tone by switching the moving components of the throat into different positions. If you think it sounds funny, don't worry about it. Remember you're just assembling the instrument, later you can make it sound any way you want. Once the "ahh" part of the diphthong is comfortable add the "ee" part of it to the end for the complete "i." Try to maintain the "dropped larynx position" during this transition. We'll go into that a bit more later. Once this exercise is comfortable, move it throughout your range.

Sing the "ahh" on a comfortable pitch in your range, complete the steps mentioned above, move the pitch one half step (probably ascending for starters) then finish the vowel by adding the "ee" to the end of it for a complete "i" (ahhh ee) take a deep breath and repeat.

This is really the sort of exercise that can help you begin to navigate the moving mechanics in the throat. Do these deliberate sustained tones for a few minutes with each vocal workout. By practicing these very physical exercises you will not only be teaching your body how to fully maneuver your instrument, but, just as importantly, teaching your ear how to recognize what these physical changes sound like.

THE SINGER'S SMILE

The *singer's smile* is just a little moderate shaping of the mouth for cleaner, purer vowels in order to create a larger exit for the big colorful tone we wish to produce.

Listen now to example on **Volume Two** recording.

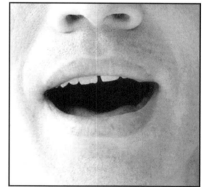

ex. 9a - Singer Smile

Without adding any tension in your face, simply curl the lips upward into a little smile (see ex 9a and 9b). It's that simple. This will open and change the shape of what is ultimately the exit for your tone. Experiment with this shape change and really listen to the difference it makes in your tone. This mouth shape will work perfectly for the vowels "a" (which is a diphthong comprised of "eh" as in "left", and "e" as in "see" ....ehhhh ee), "e" which is a vowel and "i" (which is a diphthong comprised of "ah" as in plot and and "e" as in me ... ahhhh-ee). I'm explaining diphthongs briefly at this point because it is very common to hear a singer trying to sing between the two vowels that make up a diphthong. This makes for a very muddy delivery. If you'll just try and sing one vowel at a time, I think you'll be amazed at how much easier it is to do.

The trick to well-articulated vowels lies more in the ear than in the shape of the mouth. You must articulate your vowels inside of your mouth first. Then a moderate amount of shaping can be a wonderful finishing touch. In this system, you are definitely looking for "minimal mouth movement." This will translate to

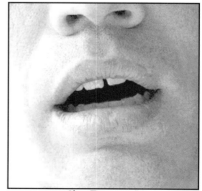

ex. 9b - Droopy Lips

more natural articulation and eliminate the possibilities for excess tensions that occur with exaggerated mouth movement.

ADDING UMB SOUND TO LIP ROLL EXERCISE

The *umb sound* is basically a completely dropped larynx *chest tone*. This is a *tone isolation exercise* perfect for warming up the extreme top end of the singing range. Spend a little time (in your comfortable middle range) putting the dropped larynx and Lip Roll exercise together. The result should be a very quiet, dull tone behind extremely slow rolling lips. Also, pay attention that your tongue stays grooved, forward and down while practicing the Lip Roll with the *umb sound.* To do this, you'll need to take your sensibilities inside your mouth to feel and hear what your tongue is doing. Once this is comfortable in your middle range begin moving this exercise upward into your upper middle range, your top singing range, and then finally the extreme top of your upper range.

The higher in your range, the harder it will be to maintain the true *umb sound.* If the tone begins to get bright then you are slipping out of the dropped larynx chest tone and into the *mouth horn*. Backup and keep practicing by looping (doing the same thing over and over again) one area of your range at a time; there's never any use in racing through an exercise.

If the Lip Roll still hasn't come together by now, you can add the *umb sound* (dropped larynx) to the Tongue Roll. Do to the position of the tongue however, it is difficult to get as deeply into the *chest resonance chamber* with the Tongue Roll as it is with the Lip Roll.

If you can do both the Tongue Roll and the Lip Roll, but your Tongue Roll is still too fast (something I call "too forward"), then add a bit of dropped larynx to it. This should both slow the tongue down, and pull your tone back "off your face" and more *backwards into your body* (something we'll talk more about later). If either the Tongue Roll or the lip Roll are still too airy, try adding some "closed nasal" to the tone. Produce this tone by saying, "stuffy nose" repeatedly to feel your nasal passage close (behind the uvula). Once you can produce this *closed nasal tone* on a *number one ratio*, then add it to the Tongue Roll, the Lip Roll, and anywhere you need it right now to help you lock into a number one ratio. We'll talk more about the *closed nasal tone* in Volume Three.

Listen now to example of "Adding the Umb Sound to The Lip Roll" on **Volume Two** recording.

Begin by using sustained tones and slowly moving upward. Then begin practicing moving this exercise over the first five notes of the major scale. We'll make it more challenging after you're comfortable with the technique.

Warming up and working out in singing is about something I call *turning on the switches.* The *switches* in the voice involve all of the different mechanical components that make it tick. An exercise like this one truly helps you turn those *switches* on. This exercise should help you think about singing *backwards into your body.* This concept is paramount for good vocal hygiene and for those wishing to sing with the big fat tone that the great singers sing with. Again, don't confuse this strange tone with style. This is purely a technique/mechanics warmup and workout exercise. Have fun.

It is important at this point that you understand two concepts:

RESONANCE FOLLOWS PITCH & REVERSE RESONANCE PSYCHOLOGY

Resonance follows pitch simply states that as you move upward in your pitch, your resonance will follow you by either getting bright and releasing through the *mouth horn* (falsetto) or in the case of many supposed accomplished singers by remaining entirely in the nasal cavity for that, oh so common "head voice" type of tone. As you descend downward the resonance will follow you into your chest which is why nine out of ten fairly good singers have no projection value on the bottom of their singing range. *Resonance follows pitch* is also responsible for multi-register singing, where you hear the distinct register breaks from low, to middle, to high in the singer that can be eliminated with a solid understanding of one register singing.

Reverse resonance psychology is simply retraining your ear and your body to pull your resonance down (into your body) as you ascend in pitch (the higher you sing, the harder you must pull down) and to pull your resonance up (into your head), the lower in pitch you sing. Adding the *umb sound* to the Lip Roll exercise is a great *reverse resonance* exercise (keeping in mind that it is only an exercise, not to be confused with style or singing). You will understand this as you find yourself working harder and harder to keep the tone dull, as you ascend into your extreme upper range. After some practice, it will become much easier and soon you will understand the importance of mastering this technique.

SING SOME MELODIES IN THE CHEST TONE

Listen now to example on **Volume Two** recording.

This is just a good way to coordinate the dropped larynx, chest tone, to the real life, less controlled environment of a melody with words. This will sound strange, but really try to stay loyal to this tone for the duration of a song. That should prove to be a challenging workout.

THE ONE BREATH EXERCISE

This is a good endurance exercise to be sung in one phrase, with *continuous energy* from one breath. Begin on a *number two ratio* in your comfortable middle range. Begin by moving this exercise downward until you enter the *no note district*. Then change over to a *number one ratio* and begin ascending as far up as you can comfortably go (this should of course be further and further with practice).

Listen now to example on **Volume Two** recording.

From the major scale this exercise sounds like: (Start by descending from the top of the scale.)

Hi – Hi – Hi – Hi – Hi – Hi – Hi – Hi – Hi – Hi – Hi – Hi
Do – Sol – Mi – Re – Fa – Mi – Sol – Fa – La – Sol – Ti – Do

LIFE ON THE BOTTOM

Since your going to take the *One Breath Exercise* down to the bottom of your range, you can now begin thinking about *reverse resonance psychology*. When you get down to the *no note district*, turn the exercise around, and begin ascending with it. Be sure and switch over to the *number one ratio* for the remaining duration of the exercise. Now, on the bottom, notes of the exercise begin to really "pull" your resonance up into your *nasal horn* (in varying degrees). This should really illustrate how you will achieve *life on the bottom* in your singing. It is, of course, achieved by *reverse resonance*. When you're down at this point in your range there will be plenty of chest resonance in your tone already. So amaze yourself and begin to balance out your tone by pulling up.

Listen now to **Volume Two** recording for example of Life On The Bottom .

The example on the Volume Two recording, not only illustrates the advantages to using a *number one ratio* and pulling your resonance up while singing on the bottom, but also highlights the unique differences between the *ratios* and resonance placements. The tone with the higher resonance and the *number one ratio* has more life and projection, while the tone with the airier *ratio* and lower resonance has a rich, woody quality to it. The point is, to play with as many tone colors as you can. They all have their place.

THE HIGH SIGH
(MouthHorn Isolation)

This is another *tone isolation exercise* concentrating primarily on the *mouth horn*. This tone will be bright (falsetto like) in your upper range and sweet and soft in your lower range.

Listen to example on **Volume Two** recording.

In a swooping fashion on the word "hi" (sounds like "haaaa-ee"), begin in your upper range and "sigh" downward as low as possible. As the exercise becomes more and more comfortable, try to start from higher and higher each time and swoop down lower and lower. This is a nice gentle way to cover your entire range. Pay close attention that you stay in the *mouth horn*. It will be very obvious if, as you descend into your lower range, you *switch* your resonance into one of the other resonance chambers. Keep the tone smooth and sweet. Also keep your tongue grooved for this exercise and maintain the *singer's smile*.

Once the *High Sigh* is comfortable, sing a few songs entirely in the *mouth horn*. The result should be a very soft, sweet delivery. You can't really get any size out of the *mouth horn* by itself, so don't push it. If, at this point, your hearing any *throat rattle* or *throat distortion* (the rattling of phlegm in your throat) then you are over-singing. Back off! This is just another exercise in control and coordination. If you can achieve the level of control necessary to remain loyal to each *resonance chamber* throughout your singing range, then your ability to tap into any or all of these resonance chambers upon command will be greatly increased.

SCRATCH TAPE

Now's the time to really start listening back to yourself on a basic recording of one kind or another. It is always a surprise for singers to hear themselves for the first several times on a recording. This is because what you hear while your singing is so different from what the listener or recorder hears. The outside listeners are not connected to your body. Think about it! Your sound producing mechanism (your voice) is housed in the same body as your sound receiving mechanism (your ears). Therefore, there is so much vibration happening internally that is, of course, going to be very different from what the external listener hears.

So, by recording and listening back to yourself doing both exercises and singing, you can begin to assimilate the true sound being produced. It will take some time, and you may even think the sound strange or even disagreeable for awhile, but it will become familiar and even comfortable soon enough. As you listen back to yourself, begin to register how these techniques you're learning really sound. Think of the individual techniques as spices. By themselves they are strange, but when mixed with other spices and prepared properly they can be wonderful. So, at this point, use the *scratch tape* on a very regular basis. Cheaper tape decks (i.e. portable cassette decks, boom boxes, etc.) alter the overall tonal qualities and very often make even the most amazing voices sound strange. Bearing this in mind, they can still be very useful as a tool to analyze your progress with vocal mechanics.

EXTREME REVERSE RESONANCE WITH ONE BREATH EXERCISE

Because our ears are conditioned to hearing *resonance follow pitch* in the majority of the world's singers, it is very easy to fool most ears by singing one pitch in the three different *resonance chambers* (as in *Resonance Shifting*). Try it. It will sound as though the pitch were moving. For that reason it is important that we recondition our ears to maintaining a more balanced resonance. To achieve this balance we must first become a little extreme in our practice. For this purpose, I would like you to now use the *One Breath Exercise* that we learned earlier and try to reverse the resonance so much that an outside listener would be very confused as to which direction the pitch were traveling in.

Listen to **Volume Two** recording for example.

Use the "hi" (sounds like "haaa-ee") word again.

Remember the break-down of this exercise on the major scale sounds like:

Do Sol Mi Re Fa Mi Sol Fa La Sol Ti Do
The resonance break down should sound like:

Hi	Hi	Hi	Hi	Hi	Hi	Hi	Hi	Hi	Hi	Hi	Hi
Chst	Chst	Chst	Nsl	Chst	Nsl	Chst	Nsl	Chst	Nsl	Chst	Chst

This is a slightly extreme yet fun ear reconditioning exercise. It should also help develop an extremely flexible sense of mechanics.

THE MIXO EXERCISE

The distance from one note to another in music is referred to as an interval. It is important to begin increasing the distance of the intervals in your practice to further prepare you for the real world of singing. The *Mixo Exercise* is a good distance/endurance exercise that can now be added to the Lip Roll Exercise. If, at this point, the Lip Roll exercise has proven impossible for you, then add it to the Tongue Roll exercise.

Listen to **Volume Two** recording for example.

ex. 10 Chicken Wing Posture

Add *Chicken Wing Posture* to the exercise (See ex. 10). This is a friendly reminder to "open up your posture" and to stay tall in the body to allow freedom for your upper ab's and diaphragm to give you the support you need for high level singing (See Diagram 10).

Using the Lip Roll and maintaining the *umb sound* practice the exercise full range. The breakdown from the major scale would be:

Do Re Mi Fa Mi Re Mi Re Do Re Ti Sol....

then back up to Do....then move up one half step and repeat.

Start in your comfortable middle range then move upwards to the extreme top. This should be a great workout exercise.

CENTERING THE PITCH

Many singers struggle with their "intonation," which means singing "in tune," or with good "pitch". Much of this is caused by mechanical problems (i.e. poor breath support or throat constriction), but much of it is caused by an undeveloped musical ear. You don't have to become a jazz theoretician to have a "good ear," but a little (or even a lot) of ear training never hurt anyone. For now, let's stick to pitch. It is common for a beginning singer to not notice their own poor intonation for awhile. Many accomplished musicians trying their hand at singing for the first time can hear their poor intonation, but cannot fix it, even after addressing many of the mechanical possibilities causing the problem. This next exercise is designed to heighten the awareness of all singers regardless of level and help in *centering the pitch*.

To practice *Centering the Pitch*, I like to use what I call *The Fluttering Exercise*. Use any instrument available (ideally one tuned to an "A" 440 reference pitch), or a recording of sustained tones covering as much of your range as possible. First, match pitches to the best of your ability, then intentionally flatten the pitch from your voice. Listen for a fluttering sound (often referred to as "beats" by guitar players). The fluttering sound is created by the pitches being just out of sync. This is the same sound you hear between strings while tuning a guitar, piano or any other stringed instrument. Try not to slide down to the next note in the scale, but deliberately try to sing between the notes. That's how you'll actually learn to hear when you're not in the *center of the pitch,* but are instead "sharp" or "flat." After you can intentionally "flatten" the pitch, slide back up into the *center of the pitch.* Repeat this exercise by now intentionally "sharpening" the pitch, to hear a nice *flutter,* then slide back down to the center. Move this exercise throughout your range to see where its easiest and where its most difficult for you. This will teach you to "tune" your ear. Then you will have good intonation. And that's a good thing.

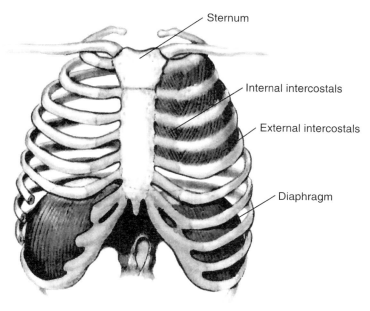

Diagram 10

THE PING PONG EXERCISE

The *Ping Pong Exercise* is a wonderful ear training exercise based off of the major scale. It was taught to me a million years ago by a former composition teacher of mine, Richard Schumacher. It has been very helpful to me and to the many singers to whom I have taught it. Music is like a bunch of roads going in all directions. An ear training exercise like this one is a road map. The more of these you put in your head, the more choices you will hear when participating in music. Go for it!

By now if you do not have the major scale woven into your brain make an effort to do so. It is a great tool and many musical benefits can be derived by knowing it. If you don't understand how it should sound ask someone to show it to you on an instrument or record it for you on a scratch tape for reference.

The major scale is: Do Re Mi Fa Sol La Ti Do

Learn it forwards and backwards. It's not that difficult.

The "Ping Pong Exercise" is

Do Re Do Mi Do Fa Do Sol Do La Do Ti Do Do (The last interval being an Octave).

Once that is comfortable do the exercise backwards:

Do Do (octave) Do Ti Do La Do Sol Do Fa Do Mi Do Re Do

Once that is comfortable begin pivoting from every position in the scale.

For example: **Re Do Re Mi Re Fa Re Sol Re La Re Ti Re Do** And then backwards:

Re Do Re Ti Re La Re Sol Re Fa Re Mi Re Do

And then: **Mi Do Mi Re Mi Fa Mi Sol Mi La Mi Ti Mi Do** Etc Etc.

YOUR NEW ROUTINE

Of course, it is impossible to practice every exercise you're learning every day. Many of the exercises in this Volume have dealt with learning specific techniques (i.e. Tongue Position and *Fluttering*). Once you have spent the necessary time needed to learn those techniques, you may then just incorporate them into your other exercises and singing. As for the rest of the exercises, use them routinely to warm up and workout before actual singing. They can be improved upon for ever and ever. Stay humble, and turn those switches on before you sing. You will not only feel a lot better during singing, but I guarantee you will also sound a lot better.

We're still using our primary exercises from Volume One. We just need to structure things now so that you can keep including new material that needs to be worked.

1. Drool Exercise with Seven Points of Relaxation 2 minutes
2. Way Down Exercise 2 minutes
3. Timed Sustained Tongue Rolls 2 minutes
4. Tongue Roll Mm Ahh exercise 1 minute
5. Timed Sustained Lip Roll 2 minute
6. Lip Roll Mm Ahh exercise 1 minute
7. Lip Roll with Umb Sound and Chicken Wing Posture using the Mixo Exercise full range 3-5 minutes
8. Resonance Shifting exercise 1 minute
9. Sustained tones on "High" with high tongue, then Grooved Tongue, then add Dropped Larynx, then move exercise 1-2 minutes
10. High Sigh exercise 1 minute
11. One Breath exercise on a Number Two Ratio from middle range down to the No Note District, then change directions and ascend on a Number One Ratio as high as possible. Stay comfortable and relaxed. Message Jaw Hinge and Root of Tongue quite a lot as you enter your upper range. This is to work out any tension that may be developing there. 2-3 minutes
12. One Breath Exercise as Extreme Reverse Resonance exercise 1-2 minutes

So far we have a 19-24 minute workout. Not bad. Now start off with some light singing on a *number two ratio* working gently towards a *number one ratio*. Then, begin playing with your *resonance shifting*. So far, we have mostly worked our resonance vertically. For now, I would like you to think mainly along those lines. In the subsequent volumes, we will spend a lot of time thinking more omni-directional with our resonance.

You should be warmed up and feeling pretty good now, so sing for as long as you have time. Still, keep it comfortable.

It is now that I'd like for you to begin to think of the *Four Parts to a Singing Session.*

THE FOUR PARTS TO A SINGING SESSION

This is an excellent order to structure your workout in for maximum efficiency of time and effort.

1. Preliminary warm-up
2. Exercise/workout period
3. Warm-up singing
4. Full singing

Part One is your preliminary warm-up. This is where you loosen up, relax, and coordinate your voice to effortlessly navigate your entire range. The voice in Part One of your warm-up is still in *the ease* stage, and should consist of the first handful of exercises you have learned, done in the order that you learned them in.

1. Drool Exercise
2. Way Down Exercise
3. Tongue Roll in its various forms
4. Lip Roll in its various forms
5. A Tone Exercise such as the One Breath Exercise done full range still focusing on The Ease

Part Two of the *Four Parts To a Singing Session* is the exercise/work-out stage. This is where you begin to think of your practice session as a workout. It is here that you focus deliberately on techniques at which you are chipping away. I've tried to cover that necessity by loading up your Volume Two routine, but in the following volumes (Volumes Three and Four) you will be learning a new series of advanced techniques that will need a lot of focus. It is important to be fully warmed up before trying the advanced techniques. This is important for both your vocal hygiene and your ability to effectively execute the techniques. And, since you will not be able to practice all of your advanced techniques in every session, you will need to be disciplined enough to mix them up and in effect rotate them (This will make complete sense after you've worked through Volume Three). For now, you could fill Part Two of your session with the *Ping Pong* exercise, *Centering the Pitch*, and a lot of *Sustained Tones* throughout your range, experimenting with the different mechanics techniques you know so far. This is truly the part of the singing session that will yield the most noticeable improvement and continued growth throughout your singing career.

Part Three of the singing session is "warm-up singing." Singing and exercising are two different worlds. Even the most demanding exercises are done in a very controlled manner. Exercises are repetitive and predictable. However, our objective is singing. And singing is far less controlled and predictable. There are varying melodies, rhythms and words which contain constantly changing vowels, consonants and meanings. So, no matter how warmed up you might be, the transition from exercises to singing can be a clunky one if not approached properly. It took me years to figure this out. I could be thoroughly warmed up and exercising on the biggest and most sophisticated techniques I could do, and yet when I began to sing, I would choke and gag on the songs. So, back off and sing a couple of warm up songs starting out on a *number two ratio* until it feels comfortable, then move to a *number three ratio* to stimulate the support system, then move to a *number one ratio* to anchor well and manage the throat pressure. After you've learned the advanced techniques from Volume Three, increase the size and energy of your singing. This warm-up singing section won't take long, because you're already warmed up from the exercises. But the fluidity you'll gain from it will astound you.

Part Four of a singing session is full-on singing. This should feel awesome at this point. Being this in touch with your voice is another place to see amazing improvement in your singing. This is a good point to have a hero or two that you want to sing along with. Through Volume Two, the difficulty level of that singer should be kept to a moderate level. After working with the higher volumes, the difficulty level should be increased to warrant experimentation and mastering of the advanced techniques. Keep the stereo playback volume down fairly low, as it is most important at this point that you listen to yourself. You are not singing along with another singer to imitate them. You are using them as a guide. When singing along with them you should be experimenting with the techniques you now know, to achieve your own desired results. If those results include imitating their sound, then it should be pursued as an experiment in vocal mechanics. Already, you have learned enough to break down a lot of the mechanics you hear in other singers. The following volumes will make it possible for you to hear and execute even the much more complex singing you hear your favorite singers doing.

If you have a small amount of time, break these four parts into equal segments. For example, if you only have forty minutes, do equal parts of ten minutes. Anything beyond that, add to parts two and four as this is where you will see the greatest improvement. Therefore, a sixty minute session would be ten minutes of Part One, twenty minutes of Part Two, ten minutes of Part Three, and twenty minutes of Part four.

If you're in command of the techniques covered in Volumes One and Two of *The Art of Body Singing*, please advance to Volumes Three and Four. It is in those volumes that you will begin to increase the energy level, size and dimension of your singing.

Hope to see you there.

Breck Alan

Please visit Bodysinging.com to purchase easy to follow routine CDs of the exercises contained in this book.

THE
ART
OF
BODY
SINGING

VOLUME III

INTRODUCTION: THE MACHETE LEVEL

Welcome back to *The Art of Body Singing,* Volume Three. This volume assumes that you've worked your way through Volumes One and Two. You'll need the foundation and vocabulary established in those two volumes to comprehend the following material. I call this "the machete level." The "bite, kick, scratch" volume. That is to say that by the time you reach this volume you are committed to becoming a serious vocalist. You'll need that commitment and patience to learn the material contained here. This material is comprised of the nuts and bolts mechanics that excellent singers are made of. Just as in Volumes One and Two, this is not about style, but about technique. Once you thoroughly understand and can execute these techniques you will have the resources to sing whatever you wish to sing, however you wish to sing it.

I remember an experience I had more than once as a music student in various music schools. I often heard the words, "musicians on this side of the room and singers on the other side of the room." It generally made me angry to not be considered a musician as a voice student. Perhaps these experiences helped motivate me to work harder. Singers often get a bad rap because singers often deserve a bad rap. As front person in a band, it's easy to misinterpret all of the attention one is given. Considering, after all, that this is the "entertainment business," a good performer is worth a lot. But when you close your eyes and listen, what's the quality level like? At the end of the day both things are important, and the only way to get a serious sound is to take the music and the instrument you're making the music with, seriously.

SINGING BACKWARDS INTO THE BODY

This concept has to do with resonance and *throat pressure*. It is so common to hear a singer really pushing and shoving when they're trying to get size from their voice. The result, of course, is that they end up singing *through their throat* and severely hindering their tone (something I call *rushing the tone*) as well as jeopardizing their vocal health. As you've heard me say in earlier volumes, you can not sing *through your throat*. You must learn to think and feel yourself singing "behind" and "over" your throat. You will gain so much size and color in your tone, if you can just back off. Involve your body, as opposed to *rushing the tone* by forcing it *through your throat* and not having the patience to hold back and search for more resonance. It is also very common to see a singer struggling with vocal health problems when trying to sing big as a result of *over-pressurizing* their vocal cords.

There are two ways to over-pressurize the vocal cords during phonation. One is by constriction in the throat. We, of course, covered this subject at length in Volume One. The other way to is by something I call *bottle necking*. That simply means to push as much air through your throat during phonation as possible. The direct result of *bottle necking* is oversinging by singing through your throat. Really make it your job to listen for those obvious signs of singing through your throat, *throat rattle* and *throat distortion*, that were described in earlier volumes. When these signs appear, back off and really think about what you already know about resonance. We will be adding some great techniques for big singing very soon, but they are of little use if you are still pushing. If you are still pushing really review and work your posture (a lifelong pursuit for many singers).

Remember the goal of the posture we're working on in *The Art of Body Singing* is one of alignment so that the support system can work freely from a reflex basis. If you are pushing, then you are trying to be too controlling of the muscles involved in the support system (described at length in Volume One). Spend more time aligning and opening up your body so that the "support system" can work freely. "Open" and "freedom" are big words in big singing. If you are "pushing" then you are trying to bully your singing. I can promise you from experience that your voice has a will of its own and will not submit (for very long at least) to being bullied. There is a huge leap of faith needed about now to believe the concept of *singing backwards into your body*. So many singers sing from the throat up, with the result being a very forced delivery and a very small *circle of tone* (something we'll talk a lot about soon). Even singers that do manage to relax and not push, but are still singing from the throat up, will always have a skinny tone that sounds as though they are *speaking the melody*. It may sound genuine and natural enough, but it just doesn't have that real "going for it" quality that belongs to the singer tapping into the big tone.

Constantly reintroduce the *seven points of relaxation* during your singing session. This will help you feel and eliminate the tensions that sneak in on you while your concentrating on one of the several other things to be thinking about during your practice session. Our obvious goal is for all of the mechanical technique we are developing to become automatic during performance. This is achieved through time, practice and patience.

RATIO SHIFTING

This is a great exercise to take your focus inside your throat and feel yourself navigating the *throat pressure switch* between the *three ratios*. It is also a wonderful way to begin developing a sense of *Dynamic Breathing*. That is to say that for the same energy level you will hear your tone size change as a result of *Ratio Shifting*. Once this exercise is comfortable, adding it to your singing is the next logical step.

Listen to the example on **Volume Three** recording.

On a comfortable pitch in your lower middle range (men start somewhere around a D below Middle C and women start somewhere around an F below Middle C. If this F is too low for you, use the men's example and follow it an octave higher), using "hi" (sounds like high) begin on a *number three ratio* and seamlessly navigate your way towards a *number one ratio* and then back to a *number three ratio*. Move the pitch and repeat, ultimately covering your full range. Listen for and teach yourself to eliminate any clunk that might be happening between *ratios*. This clunkiness is inevitably a result of pushing with the support system, a lack of even support, or a general lack of good throat pressure management. Remember that the throat pressure will change when shifting between ratios, and it is your job to control that pressure and, of course, never allow it to exceed *conversation level throat pressure*. Use *throat rattle* and *throat distortion* as an indication of oversinging. Pulling your resonance back and down will help manage this and eliminate clunkiness. Also, keep reviewing your big, open posture. The more you practice *Ratio Shifting*, the smoother it will become. This will prove to be a very valuable technique in singing with good tone variety.

SINGING OFF THE BREATH

Listen to example on **Volume Three** recording.

Really pay attention to your breathing patterns in singing. It is very common to hear a singer holding their breath just before singing a phrase. When you hold your breath, your throat automatically begins to constrict to keep the air from escaping through the trachea. Therefore, if you are holding your breath before a phrase you are beginning your singing from an already constricted throat. So begin teaching yourself to sing (or speak) directly from the inhale. You will be amazed at how this will free up your throat. Developing the timing for this task is simply a matter of practice.

This concept can also be applied to avoid the throat constriction that happens to a singer in mid-phrase. If your support system is producing X amount of air and control at the beginning of a phrase, your throat is prepared for that particular amount. If in mid-phrase, the support begins to diminish, it is very common for the throat to begin to constrict around the smaller volume of air. This is poor management from both departments. For one, you should not be singing on such auto pilot to allow your throat to constrict at any time. Secondly, if your support system is diminishing support mid-phrase, then you are probably collapsing your open rib cage position, and therefore strangling your support system. It is also common to hear a singer *rationing their energy*. Although you are working very hard here not to push with your support system you must still be very continuous with your energy. Focus on something across the room from where you're singing. Think of your continuous energy as moving forward to connect with that object. If you ration your energy, there will be holes in that connection. So, even though we're singing *backwards into our body*, we must think forward with our energy.

FAST AIR

This technique will allow you to graduate out of lower energy level (*the ease*) you've been working in, and into *high energy* singing, without compromising the good vocal hygiene you've been working so hard (in Volumes One and Two) to achieve.

To better understand this concept called *Fast Air*, I like to explain it through three titles.

THREE TITLES FOR FAST AIR

1. *Fast Air*
2. *Energy Air*
3. *Deceptive Air*

1. This technique is called *Fast Air*, because there is an audible increase in the speed and amount of the air from your support system. You must use a very special technique to achieve this, so that you do not allow yourself to over-sing, by singing *through the throat*.

2. This technique is called *Energy Air*, because now that you've worked so hard on coordinating the mechanics of your voice, you are ready to begin increasing the *energy* level. This is what will take you into the *Big Singing* you've been working up to.

3. This technique is called *Deceptive Air*, because even though you are increasing the amount of air and energy you are using, you must remember that much of the *Fast Air* technique, is just that, a technique. It is truly deceptive how much air is really coming out of your throat during this technique

Listen to **Volume Three** recording for example of Fast Air.

Practice *fast air* using sustained tones on "hi" (sounds like "high"), throughout your range. Stay on the *number three ratio* for now. Think very up with the air, directing it into the nasal passage. This will yield several positive results involving resonance as well as air placement. Stay on a *number three ratio* until you have complete command of this technique. It should sound very bright. If the tone has a thick "h-ee" quality, you are pushing *through the throat*. Again, think up with the air and that should relieve any excess *throat pressure*. The air should certainly have the illusion of moving very fast. The faster the air, the bigger your mouth and the more grooved your tongue should be (see *mouth sizing* below). This makes for an ease in delivery by opening from the tone passage outward. Also, remember to keep checking yourself with the *Candle Theory* (see *Candle Theory* below). If at any point, you are feeling any scorching or fatigue in the throat then you are doing the technique incorrectly. Re-listen to the examples on the recording and keep trying to find the exact feeling of doing this exercise correctly. When this is comfortable, try this technique with some songs you know. This technique, with a number three ratio, should prove to be a great workout. Have fun.

THE CANDLE THEORY

As a safety measure in using this new technique, I would like you to use what's called the *Candle Theory* as a guide in your singing. The *Candle Theory* means this: no matter how big, energetic, high in your range, or regardless of ratio you're singing on, you should never be able to blow out a small candle placed directly in front of your mouth. You don't need to burn yourself experimenting with this technique. Simply place your fingers directly in front of your mouth while singing and imagine they are a small candle. You can flicker the candle (although not very much), but you can not blow it out. The same applies to the area just below your nostrils.

MOUTH SIZING

I would like you to begin incorporating *Mouth Sizing* into your singing, as you move into this new level of energy. Common sense tells us that if we wish to increase the size of our tone we must increase the size of the exit for our tone. Use your ear as your guide here. Still using the *singers smile* and the *grooved tongue position*, size your mouth in proportion to your energy level (see ex. 11). Experiment with this in front of a mirror. You'll be amazed at the difference a little *mouth sizing* can make. Still though, keep it simple and don't let this translate into any excessive mouth movement (mouthing), as this will only create tension.

PROJECTION

In singing, projection is about your song literally flying from your mouth. The two main elements in projection are tone and articulation. As you may have noticed by now, in *The Art of Body Singing* I spend a lot more time working on tone than I do working on articulation. I think, like with any system of teaching, be it singing, martial arts, cooking, or whatever, it basically reflects the creator of the system's perspective. It is my view that tone is the cornerstone for expressing emotions. For my money, a singer that has thoroughly explored their tone variety is far more interesting than a well articulated singer, singing on a "bread and butter tone," that is meant to convey every emotion in the book. Don't get me wrong, I'm a believer in articulation. I just think its a subject that can be attached fluidly to a strong foundation of mechanics via the ear. This is why I don't teach a lot of specific vowel placements. I think the ear is a much better guide once the body is on the same team. My view on how you should study diction is covered in Volume Four. And do remember, should your perspective ever be somewhat different than mine, I can accept that. The only reason *The Art of Body Singing* exists in the first place, is that I was constantly in search of a deeper understanding of the voice.

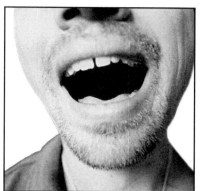

ex. 11 - Big Mouth with Singer
Smile and grooved tongue

NASAL HORN BUZZ

The nasal horn produces your most projecting tone. Learning to successfully blend this resonance with resonance from as low in your body as you can possibly reach will create your fattest tone.

The *nasal horn buzz exercise* is another *tone isolation exercise*. It is your first goal to successfully navigate your entire singing range isolated entirely in the *nasal horn resonance chamber*. This will only be possible once the utmost relaxation is achieved in the *throat pressure* department and the support-system is in complete cooperation.

Listen now to examples on **Volume Three** recording.

Use the word "French" (pronounced "freench"), to find the buzziest tone you can achieve from your *nasal horn*. Listen to the arc on the top of the word. It is at that arc you should hear the most amount of buzz. Once you can tap into that deep buzz, try and maintain it as long as you can. This will require some concentration and serious relaxation in the throat. The second you begin to over-pressurize in the throat, you will hear your tone being pulled out of the nasal horn and quite probably into the throat. (Listen for a gargling sound; this indicates constriction in the throat.)

Once you've mastered the art of entering the *Nasal Horn Buzz* via the "freench" word, begin in a comfortable area in your middle range using sustained tones on the long "e" vowel. Once this is comfortable, move these sustained tones full range. Then begin moving the exercise. Using the first five notes of the major scale, ascending, then descending, should be fine for now (do re mi fa sol fa mi re do). Really listen as you ascend higher that you don't start pulling out of the nasal horn. This is called "finishing out." Another definition for an *isolated tone* is an "unfinished tone." You will hear a significant diminish in the amount of buzz from the nasal horn, should you begin "finishing out."

Once you can stay isolated in the nasal horn, practice singing some songs in this resonance chamber. By itself the nasal horn is very harsh and annoying. But the only way to fully understand mechanics in singing, is by isolating them in your workouts on a regular basis. After spending some time isolating your three resonance chambers, it doesn't take long to see that the nasal horn is the most projecting of the three. For an equal level of energy, the nasal horn will give the illusion of a much louder tone. Ultimately, of course, you're going for some level of blend with your resonance, but I guarantee that is much easier to navigate once you've fully learned to manage each resonance chamber on its own.

TONE MARRIAGE

We've spent a great deal of time so far isolating our resonance. We've been working our resonance vertically up until now. Now comes the time when we begin to think more omni-directional with our resonance. Some systems like to call this "blending." I like to give it a bit grander definition, because I have grander expectations in mind.

I call this subject *tone marriage,* because I optimistically believe that the union of individual components can certainly make for a greater sum. Something along the lines of "mutual momentum."

I also call this same subject *tone harmony.* If you really work at hearing the involvement of all three resonance chambers in the end result of your tone, you will notice a flowering quality to the size and color of your singing. This is the same result of separate singers singing in harmony.

I also call this same subject *circle of tone.* If you work your resonance from as low in your body as possible to as high in your body as possible you will continue to increase the size of your circle.

The following two techniques, *The Half Way Technique,* and the *Percentage Technique,* should prove to be among the most effective *tone marriage* techniques that you will ever come across.

THE HALF WAY TECHNIQUE

The *half way technique* is our beginning of *tone marriage.* This technique combines a *closed nasal technique,* and a chest tone, with varying degrees of "dropped larynx."

Listen to **Volume Three** recording for example of the *closed nasal technique*

To execute the *closed nasal technique,* first begin by talking with a stuffy nose. This should sound like you have a cold. This technique is located directly at the *nasal horn.* Rather than opening the nasal horn, as you recently learned to do with the *nasal horn buzz,* you are deliberately closing this resonance chamber. The resonance produced from this technique is still a nasal cavity resonance. It is just a *closed nasal* resonance, verses an open nasal resonance. If you open your mouth fairly wide, and look in a mirror while alternating from the closed nasal technique, to the nasal horn buzz, you should see your uvula changing positions. The uvula should be very high during the *closed nasal technique*. As you open up your tone with the nasal horn buzz, you should clearly see your uvula dropping, opening up the nasal passage (see examples 12a & 12b).

The benefit that the *closed nasal technique* brings a singer, is something I call *anchoring*. This is a remarkable aid in helping singers graduate to high energy singing, without singing through the throat. The only misfortune with this technique is the amount of singers that do not graduate past it (we have already planted the seeds to graduate past it but for now you'll need to master it). Really begin listening for singers that have a very closed nasal tone. You will hear many examples. I can't tell you how many times I've heard singers tell me they sing better with a cold. This is because their nasal passage is stuffed up, and therefore, automatically closed. This forces them to stay *anchored* and really helps prevent oversinging. So, once again do not think of this as style, but as a wonderful aid in feeling ourselves *anchoring* our voices so that we may later learn to spring from this wonderful foundation. For now really spend some time trying to sing through out your range in the *closed nasal technique*. Basically handle this like another *tone isolation exercise*. Singers should be able to safely manipulate their voices in and out of the strangest techniques. So go for it.

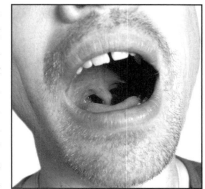

ex. 12a
Uvula down
(open nasal passage)

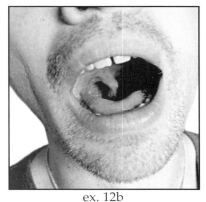

ex. 12b
Uvula high
(closed nasal passage)

Once you can easily maneuver the *closed nasal technique*, begin adding a "chest tone." Do this at first, by looking in a mirror and dropping your larynx to varying degrees. Really listen to make sure that you are adding the two resonances together, as opposed to *shifting* from one resonance to another. This should produce a rather sizable *circle of tone*, as this is the beginning of *tone marriage*. Practice this throughout your range, and really continue to *anchor* your tone with the closed nasal on top (your head),and fatten your tone with the chest tone" on bottom (your body). Stay in a *number one ratio* for now as this will make the *tone marriage* easier to hear. After some practice, you'll be amazed at how high in your range you can safely sing without changing registers. Of course, you must remember to keep pulling down into your body with your tone and keep *anchoring* at the nasal horn. This will sound very "singy" and dull at first, particularly in your lower and middle range (this is because there is no buzzy, edgy tone that comes from a more open nasal horn). Observe though how the technique begins to "naturalize" the higher in your range that you sing. This is, of course, a product of *resonance following pitch*. The higher you sing, the more resonance from the resonance chambers in your head will naturally be present. This is why you must learn to reach lower and lower in your resonance the higher you sing, and higher and higher in your resonance the lower you sing (*reverse resonance psychology*).

Listen to example on **Volume Three** recording.

Practice *The Half Way Technique* as you would any other technique. Be slow and deliberate at first. Start off with sustained tones, and as soon as that becomes comfortable begin moving the exercise. After moving over the first five notes of the major scale is comfortable, begin practicing this technique over some familiar songs. Having a few *tool songs,* that cover your entire range, is a good idea for practicing techniques. That way, as you move from one technique to another, it is over familiar material. The less to think about the better. This allows you more concentration for the technique. After spending some time with your techniques, you'll be able to slip fluidly through them all without a lot of intellectual burden. They will become attached to your sense of expression and emotion. There will always be room in your practice sessions to improve upon them, but after a certain learning curve, they will become very automatic and natural during performance.

THE SIREN

Listen to examples on **Volume Three** recording.

This is a swooping, ascending exercise (the opposite of the *high sigh*), staying locked into *The Half Way Technique.* Using a nice open vowel like "a" (sounds like "ah") begin in your comfortable lower middle range and swoop upward as high as you can possibly ascend. Stay *anchored* at the nasal horn and keep pulling down into your chest, deeper and deeper the further you ascend with *The Siren.* Stay loyal to the number one ratio. After you've ascended as far as you can possibly go, finish off the exercise by descending back down into your lower range. You should not hear any register changes or breaks with this exercise. That would be "multi-register singing." Remember, your goal is to achieve "one register singing." Then later, if you wish to break up your registers for interpretation reasons, it will be by choice rather than by default.

THE UPPER MIDDLE

The *upper middle,* is the area in your range that, when developed, will allow you to sing the most difficult material on the planet. As you know by now I truly want you to develop your entire singing range. But it is the upper middle range that really carries with it that sense of acrobatic singing. The control and energy necessary to navigate this area of your range, consistently and fluidly, is apparent not only to yourself, but to the listener. This is the area in your range above the typical singer's "breaking point." This is the most projecting area of your range. *The Half Way Technique* can help you master this part of your range, and stay connected to your body. Use it diligently for that purpose.

The area of your voice that can be easily sung without "breaking" is often referred to in classical singing as the "Tessetura." This is how voices are typically classified as basses, baritones, tenors, altos and sopranos. The key is not how many notes you can sing, but how many notes you can sing in a full, high quality voice. When someone says they wish to expand their range, what they should really be thinking about is expanding their "quality" range.

THE VOLUME DIAMOND

The *Volume Diamond* is something all acoustic instruments possess. It simply means there will be a point when an instrument is capable of *marrying* the largest possible *circle of tone,* to create the loudest possible volume. Respect this in your voice. As you're practicing your exercises make mental notes concerning your *Volume Diamond.* Also remember, volume can be very misleading. At the end of the day, it is projection that will carry your voice.

THE PERCENTAGE TECHNIQUE

This is the finishing technique for *tone marriage.* The *Percentage Technique* is about starting off in a nice *anchored, Half Way Technique,* and then beginning to open up the *nasal horn* in small increments. This adds the projecting element to the *circle of tone.* It is important to open up the nasal horn in small increments, so you will not lose the wonderful *anchoring* achieved by the *closed nasal technique.* It is also important that you experiment with varying degrees of the dropped larynx, while adding the *percentage technique* to your practicing and singing. The lower the larynx, the bigger the *circle of tone.* (This is because the dropped larynx position allows us to place our resonance deeper into our chest. This position also changes the shape of the throat, seriously changing the overall tone.) The higher the larynx, the more projecting the tone. Don't confuse a higher larynx with disconnecting from the chest tone. Although many singers do disconnect from their bodies (resulting in multi register singing), our goal is of course not to disconnect, regardless of our larynx position.

Listen to examples on **Volume Three** recording.

Begin preparing for the *Percentage Technique,* by finding the *switch* for the closed nasal and open nasal tones. Spend some time practicing switching back and forth between these techniques throughout your range. This should sound like you are switching from the *closed nasal technique,* to the *nasal horn buzz.*

Once that switch is well within your command, begin adding it to the *half way technique.* Do not open up too much or you will lose your anchor and begin singing through the throat. This is why the technique is titled the *Percentage Technique.* A little nasal horn will go along way.

Once this technique becomes comfortable, really begin experimenting with the amount of dropped larynx you use. A very dropped larynx, in conjunction with a very open nasal passage, will produce the biggest *circle of tone* possible. This becomes subjective after awhile, and it will be entirely your choice as to how much of any of the *three resonance chambers* you might like to add to your tone.

Also experiment from which direction you add resonance. For some singers it is easier to add chest resonance to existing higher resonance (i.e *nasal horn* or *mouth horn*) than vice versa. In fact, many systems of voice training spend a lot of time focusing on something called the "Masque." An equivalent term in our system would be an *open nasal anchor.* Think of this when switching back and forth from the closed nasal and open nasal tones. "LET THE BUZZ BE THE GUIDE." Once you can do this successfully and stay very anchored (not singing through the the throat) you should be able to consistently feel the *open nasal anchor* (Masque), and add the lower resonances to it. This should offer you the best of everything: an open, anchored, big circle of tone.

Practice this technique over sustained tones first, and then begin moving it, both ascending and descending, to hear and feel the effects it has throughout your singing range.

FAST AIR CRESCENDOS

This is where you get to merge the high energy level of the *Fast Air Technique* with the big circle of tone you're striving for. "Crescendos" (a dynamic change from softest to loudest) are wonderful ways to constantly search for more *tone harmony* and to explore your different energy levels. As you've been learning since the beginning, coordination is the first key in singing. Once that becomes a reality for a singer, the next step is to carefully, yet constantly, push the envelope for size and color of tone (without actually physically pushing or straining of course). Changing your energy level is an obvious necessity to achieve that goal. It is quite common to hear a singer that has learned a great deal about coordination and control, and yet will sing entire performances without changing their energy level. This tends to yield a very non-dramatic performance. We'll talk more about *energy changes* later. For now, the object is to find as high of an energy level as possible (safely), and shift your ratio to create as big of a tone as you can possibly create (safely).

Listen to examples on **Volume Three** recording.

Begin as always in a comfortable place in your range. Using our old stand-by, the "hi" word (sounds like "high"), begin on a *number three ratio* using *fast air* energy. Now, basically do a *ratio shift* (just like we learned at the beginning of this Volume), towards a number one ratio. Using all of your wonderful *tone marriage* techniques, explore with your resonance on this new high level of energy established with *energy air*. Because you have successfully learned the techniques required to execute *deceptive air*, and because you have learned to properly *anchor* your tone before opening it up with the *Percentage Technique*, there should be no oversinging even at the loudest point of these crescendos. Pushing will get you nowhere. Once all of these techniques begin to work together, you should hear a wonderful *flowering* (*tone harmony*) effect at the height of your "crescendo." Always end this exercise with a seamless "decrescendo," then move the exercise and practice it full range.

PO PA EXERCISE

This is an incredible distance exercise, that should basically be incorporated into your most difficult workouts. The *Po Pa* exercise was taught to me by a former teacher, Peter Elvins. I had not before, and have not since, worked with anyone that could get as much size and color from their voice as Peter.

The goal of this exercise should be to sing every second of it on your maximum energy level and on your maximum-sized tone. Really think of *continuous energy* with this exercise. As Peter Elvins used to say, "think of the bow of a Cello crossing the strings continually with each phrase." In other words, no breaks in the energy. Glue the consonants together and never let your energy drop. I like to think of the energy like a *wave*. The notes and words that we sing are the ships on top. If the wave drops out then the ships fall to the ocean floor. Translation, "we don't sing notes, we sing phrases." This is true whether or not we are singing something that is legato, staccato, or something in-between. Keep your energy alive.

The exercise sounds like this:

Po	Pa	Po	Pa (sustain last note, big breath, then) Po	Pa	Po	Pa
Mi	Do	Re	Sol	Sol	Re	Mi	Do

Then move the starting note a half step in whichever direction you are taking the exercise, and repeat.

Try this exercise full range. Really work your *reverse resonance* trying to keep the most balanced tone possible throughout the exercise.

STANCE NUMBER TWO

With an exercise as demanding as the *Po Pa* exercise, this is a good time to practice another stance to work your posture. Stance number two has all of the same alignment principles as stance number one (see Volume One "Posture"). To achieve this stance, bring your feet together and lean out over them as though you were about to dive off a cliff. Distribute most of your weight to the balls of your feet. Push your chest and rib cage out as far as you can without arching your back. Keep your shoulders down, slightly back and relaxed. This stance should help you focus even more than you've been doing on lifting and opening the upper torso. As you've been learning, the more open this is, the more freedom the support system has to operate on a reflex basis.

This concludes Volume Three. I hope you have really put some time into the techniques covered in this volume. If so, your confidence level should be rising to meet your ability level. Don't worry if things still sound a bit clunky. There is a real settling period with learning. The more you practice the more you will find the *switches* to master the techniques involved in singing. With time this information will begin to settle into your body, as well as your mind. As that happens, you will notice your consistency level beginning to rise. In the next volume (Volume Four), applying these techniques you've been working on is covered extensively. Not to mention some more amazing techniques for *Olympic level singing.*

Hope to meet you there.

Breck Alan

Please visit Bodysinging.com to purchase easy to follow routine CDs of the exercises contained in this book.

THE
ART
OF
BODY
SINGING

VOLUME IV

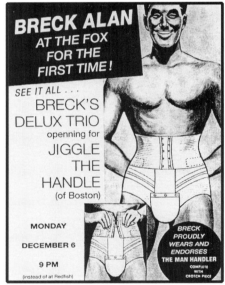

FIFTY MORE THINGS YOU SHOULD KNOW ABOUT SINGING

Listen now to Introduction of **Volume Four** recording.

This volume is fast paced and assumes that you have a strong working knowledge of the vocabulary and techniques established in Volumes One, Two and Three. Although there will be several new concepts and techniques added here, I like to think of Volume Four as the "Application Volume." You should find some wonderful ideas in this volume to further help you naturalize your singing. This process, like everything we've worked on, begins with the ear. There is a natural learning curve to be expected when you're learning a technique with any instrument or art form. When you're processing the amount of information involved in *The Art of Body Singing*, things are bound to sound a bit intellectual for awhile. But rest assured, the more you really teach yourself to own the technique, the more naturally you will be able to execute it. So, continue to chip away at your mechanics, allow for a settling period, and have fun.

THE FALSETTO PRINCIPLES

A definition of "falsetto" that I saw long ago was "false voice." Another very popular definition is "light voice above regular singing voice." In my opinion, both definitions are inadequate and slightly misleading. The main principle in "falsetto" is the the tone achieved primarily by *releasing* through the mouth horn. As you learned with the *High Sigh* tone isolation exercise in Volume Two, this effect can be achieved anywhere in your range. As you have also learned by now, it is completely feasible to sing in a fully connected voice, in your extreme upper range, without disconnecting into the *mouth horn* (i.e. "One Register Singing"). With this in mind, use your mouth horn ("falsetto") tone as a color whenever you choose. However, do not allow it to take over by default in your upper range when staying connected seems difficult. If this is still happening, you need to work harder on your *half way technique* and then on your *Percentage Technique.*

Listen to **Volume Four** recording for example.

You can customize your "falsetto" by experimenting with different *tone marriages.* For example, warm it up by dropping your larynx and adding some chest resonance to it, increase its power and projection by adding some open nasal buzz to it, or play with your *air ratios* and energy levels on it. Don't limit this bright tone to your upper range. Play with it full range. The more control you have over your tone, the more means you will have of expressing your emotions.

THE SINGER RELEASE

Listen to example on **Volume Four** recording.

The *singer release* is a deceiving embellishment using the mouth horn tone. By releasing into the mouth horn, from a more connected tone you can give the impression of more distance between intervals than actually exists. This is just one of many stylistic touches that you can add to your singing by slipping from one technique to another.

THE YI SCALE

Listen to example on **Volume Four** recording.

This is a very user-friendly singing tool for working on the bigger singing. "Yi" is a "triphthong" (three connected vowel sounds) "e," (as in "free") "a" (as in "ah") and "e" again. You might also look at this exercise as "E Ah E." Use this triphthong over whichever scales and melodies you find helpful. Definitely sing it full range and with as high of energy as you are currently ready for.

DICTION

At this point, I suggest that you invest in a good diction book. I personally like the "Singers Manual of English Diction" by Madeleine Marshall. As I have pointed out in earlier volumes, different diction books use different vocabulary. Crossing them can sometimes sound contradictory and confusing. This is one of the reasons I do not go to great depth on the subject of diction in *The Art of Body Singing*. Another reason is that there are others who have dedicated far more time to that subject than myself and are far more qualified to teach it. It should also be noted that in my view over-stringent diction requirements, particularly at an early stage in a singer's development can severely stylize their singing. It is the intention of *The Art of Body Singing* to develop singers to a place where they can truly cultivate their own personal style. With that said, I still fully encourage the advanced singer to spend some time studying diction. By learning some of the more necessary rules in this subject, you will be amazed at the amount of clunkiness you can eliminate from your singing. As we have said earlier in this system, a general rule is to *skip off the consonants* and *live on the vowels*. Dedicating some time to a more specific diction guide can fully enhance that general rule.

THE VIBRATO PRINCIPLES

Listen to example on **Volume Four** recording.

"Vibrato" is often encouraged far too early in singers. The type of "vibrato" that is most often taught to novice singers is one of fabrication and manipulation. That is to say that singers are taught to create their vibrato by pulsing their support system and/or using strange manipulations in their throats. These vibratos sound extremely fake, and personally, I have a hard time taking a performance seriously where I feel I'm being conned. Don't get me wrong, if someone has created a stylistic embellishment along the lines of a "quiver," then I have no problem with that. However, when I hear a singer extend that "quiver" over a sustained vowel, trying to pass it off as "vibrato," I can't help but be offended. Our goal in *The Art of Body Singing,* is something I call *open body vibrato*. *Open body vibrato* is the result of balancing the echoing between the resonance chambers, the evenness of the support system and the perfect level of throat pressure. *Open body vibrato* can be a wonderful guide to singing *backwards into your body* and not oversinging. By not fabricating your vibrato with the premature methods mentioned earlier, you will begin to hear *open body vibrato* appearing naturally when your coordination is at the level necessary for it to appear. Controlling this natural vibrato is done by experimenting with your resonance placement and by varying the amount of pressure created by the support system. For example, if you are hearing a fast vibrato that is emitting mostly from the head, you might experiment by placing your resonance lower in your body and backing off on your support system pressure. This should produce a slower vibrato that is centered more in the body than in the head. There are, of course, many possibilities for a controlled and customized *open body vibrato*. Beware that if you are still pushing *through your throat,* you will find it very difficult to produce anything other than a fabricated vibrato. This is because you are still *rushing the tone*. Find your "back off switch" and be amazed at how the tone blossoms.

THREE PARTS TO A NOTE

Listen to example on **Volume Four** recording.

The *three parts to a note* are the beginning, middle and the end. Use what I call the *ease in* and *ease out* techniques to clearly distinguish between the *three parts to a note*. To do this, let the air gently lead the way until the initial tone is created by the vocal cords, and then supported by resonance. Be very deliberate at first and make this sound like a little crescendo. This should severely eliminate any clunkiness you might still be hearing on your entries and exits of notes. Once this is natural for you, begin to shorten these entries and exits depending upon interpretation.

TWO PARTS TO THE MIDDLE

Listen to example on **Volume Four** recording.

Two parts to the middle, has to do with *living on the vowel*. At this point, you should be very comfortable with sustaining vowels. *Two parts to the middle,* is a concept that simply asks that you experiment playing around with that vowel to create a sense of life in the performance. Many singers take this too far and try to demonstrate every technique they know with every song. I think it far more believable to find the character the song wants, and maintain it. *Two parts to the middle* simply teaches you a nice tool to add nuance to that character without going overboard. Try changing the middle of a sustained tone by changing your resonance, your ratio, your energy etc., during that sustained vowel.

ARTICULATION

Listen to example on **Volume Four** recording.

So much of this subject should go under the heading of common sense. Listen to yourself. If you can't understand what you're saying then neither can anyone else. If you want to improve your articulation, begin in the mouth. This is where the "articulators" (tongue, lips and teeth) will be found. Stick to our earlier rule of *minimal mouth movement*. You will only distort your articulation and add unwanted tensions by excessive mouth movement. Think "inside your mouth" and "forward," out of the throat with articulation. This is where purity in articulation will be achieved. Then, connect this *forward articulation* with the fat tone achieved by singing *backwards into the body*. Because articulation is another large factor in projection, its development, along with the tone development you've been working so hard on, will prove to be an amazing partnership. Much will be learned about articulation by your study of diction.

PULSING PROJECTION

Listen to example on **Volume Four** recording.

This concept is basically about the effectiveness of "emphasis." You've worked very hard in the past three volumes to create an amazing level of control and evenness in your singing. The intent is that once control and evenness can be achieved, then so can safe, effective recklessness. In this exercise, simply emphasize every other note by increasing the volume (which can most effectively be done by increasing the energy or singing a less airy tone). Once you've spent a little time playing with this concept, you'll be amazed at how easily it will fall into place with your singing. Hearing this executed, in a natural manner, has a great effect on the projection and overall life of the piece being sung.

ENERGY CHANGES

It is far too common to hear a singer that has become comfortable with their mechanics, to sing on such an even keel that there is no variation in the energy of their delivery. This can unfortunately make for an uninspiring performance. Therefore, it is important that once you have your mechanics working for you, that you begin to develop your sense of *energy changes*, resulting in something I like to think of as *dynamic breathing*. The following exercise *number two crescendos*, should help cultivate your sense of *energy changes*.

NUMBER TWO CRESCENDOS

Listen to example on **Volume Four** recording.

A favorite exercise of mine, for both warming up and developing a sense of *energy changes*, is something I call *number two crescendos*. These are basically crescendos done from start to finish on a *number two ratio*. What this means is that you can't rely on your *ratio shifting* to provide the crescendo for you. You must increase your energy to create the crescendo, and decrease your energy to create the decrescendo. This should really get you in touch with your energy switch. Since *air plus resonance equals tone*, it is obvious that what you are increasing is your air. It is important that as this happens you don't allow yourself to sing *through the throat*. You must manage this increased energy and turn it into more resonance not additional throat pressure. Think of your technique as changing from *the ease* level of energy into a *fast air* level of energy. And remember with *number two crescendos*, to stay loyal to the number two ratio.

THREE WAYS TO CRESCENDO

Since crescendoing and decrescendoing, are something you will constantly be doing in your singing to create a sense of *dynamic breathing*, you need to be aware of the *three ways to crescendo*. Those three ways are:

1. Change your ratio to a more fully supported ratio (i.e. less airy).
2. Increasing your energy.
3. Increasing your circle of tone.

SPEAKING WITH THREE INTENSITIES

You have learned from the beginning that speaking and singing are first cousins. Now would be a good time to translate some of your high level singing skills, to high level speaking. Understanding this concept should develop an increased awareness of *energy changes*, *dynamic breathing* and projection.

Listen to example on **Volume Four** recording.

The three intensities for speaking are:

1. Conversational Level
2. Across the Room Level
3. Shakespearean Level

Practice this exercise over just about any sentence from your normal speaking voice. For now, think of all of the three intensities on a number one ratio. This will make discerning energy levels and projection easier.

With *conversation level speaking,* your energy can be very low and projection is only of moderate importance. Articulation is probably the more important subject. If you have mastered the *number one ratio* then *conversational level speaking* should be virtually effortless.

Across the room level speaking should require an increase in energy, a bit more of an open mouth, somewhat cleaner articulation, possibly an edgier resonance, and certainly a springier projection.

Shakespearean level speaking demands everything I just listed for *across the room level speaking* and then some. You really need to feel your body open up just as you would in big singing. Your energy level will quite possibly need to be as high as it would be for your most demanding singing. You must really project your tone here, by *skipping off the consonant* and *living on the vowel*. Hear yourself articulate clearly and literally throw your words to the back of the theatre as a Shakespearean actor might do. Remember, projection means to fly. These principles will all apply to singing. As we learned very early on, the longer you *live on the vowel,* then the closer you are to singing.

THE BELTING PRINCIPLE OF CENTERING THE TONE

Singing can often be very deceptive to the underdeveloped ear. It is not uncommon for improperly trained singers to virtually yell and scream their more demanding or loudest parts. This is a good way to have a very short singing career. You must always remember that no matter how nasty, edgy, hard or loud a singer may appear to be singing, that there is always a way to achieve those results in a healthy manner. No matter what myth you may choose to believe about natural talent, any singer, who has had a long and fruitful career singing high level stuff, has paid their dues wood-shedding to develop a technique that would allow them to sing in that manner night after night, year after year.

You've spent a lot of time learning to smoothly enter a note. (entries are sometimes referred to as "the attack.") I have talked about the *three parts to a note*. You have applied the *ease in* technique to help facilitate your entries. Now I'd like to look at *centering the tone*. This basically means to land right in the center of whatever size note you intend to sing. By eliminating the *ease in,* you will add a tremendous projection value and give the impression of "belting" (which by definition is to hit the note hard). Done properly this will sound like extremely loud singing. But in reality, it will be your projection that will be cutting through the air at the speed of light (or at least at the speed of sound). Once you master *centering the tone,* you can connect it to any color of tone that you wish. Later in this volume, we will be working on a subject called *throat effects.* That is how you will learn to healthily create a tone that sounds rough and throaty. Once you have successfully navigated *throat effects,* you can couple it with *centering the tone* for the hardest, nastiest sounding singing you will ever produce. The bonus being that you will not be screaming, you will be projecting.

Listen to example on **Volume Four** recording.

Begin on a number one ratio sustained tone in your comfortable middle range. Use the "eya" sound at first to ease into the note. After this is comfortable, eliminate the "e" and center the note with "ya." Always remember that even if you aren't using the *Ease In Technique,* you must feel a *set up* in your throat, and be anchored mentally, so that you do not sing through the throat. Feeling that *set up* will always insure that you are singing behind the throat. Practice these sustained tones several times, taking your conscious thought into your throat. As subtle as it is, it is very important that you feel this *set up* along with your *throat pressure switch.* Even though you are constantly developing the minimal amount of throat pressure (*conversational level throat pressure*), it still exists and we must not ignore it. It is common for opera singers to state that they try to sing as though they have no throat. This amazing ideal is only possible once you have mastered singing *behind the throat* and *backwards into the body. Throat management* is an on going pursuit if you intend to sing healthily. So your choice is to feel it while you can manage it, or to feel the effects of oversinging.

Once you are comfortable with this technique of *centering the tone,* begin to use it on your *tool songs* and on your more ambitious exercises like the *Po Pa Exercise.*

THE THREE STEPS TO WORKING OUT A DIFFICULT PASSAGE

As with everything in *The Art of Body Singing*, there is a method behind the madness. There is no reason to struggle with singing. Just as you learned from the Four Parts to a Singing Session, process is everything. This is the process for working out a difficult passage.

> **1.** Happy Throat
> **2.** Placement
> **3.** Size

Listen to example on **Volume Four** recording.

Be very warmed up and have already finished the first three parts of a singing session.

Begin by looping the piece you're working on, one section at a time. Sing this section using as *bright* and *released* a tone as is necessary to stay comfortable. Constantly re-introduce *the seven points of relaxation* throughout the *four parts to a singing session*. You should constantly be shooting for *the drool* feeling throughout your session. After you are very relaxed and comfortable with this difficult passage, on a bright, released tone (this is step 1. *Happy Throat*), begin to pull your resonance backwards out of the *mouth horn* and into the body. Anchoring with the half way technique would be a good idea at this point. Once this is comfortable, begin to open up your tone with the percentage technique (this is step 2. *Placement*). Once this is comfortable, begin to increase your energy until you're singing at your desired level for this piece (this is step 3. *Size*). Sometimes increasing the energy level, before opening up the tone (with the percentage technique), can produce excellent results. This may help keep you from oversinging (by first keeping you anchored with the half way technique). Just don't get stuck in the more closed tone (closed nasal), as unfortunately many singers do.

Another possibility that works well for some singers is to go from the *happy throat*, to *fast air* energy while staying on a number three ratio, to a more fully supported ratio, to working placement from there. Ideally, do your high level tone work in a number one ratio, as that will help you find the biggest circle of tone possible. You can always add air on top later for effect. Experiment!

Breck's Opinion

It is completely your responsibility to maintain a healthy voice. You can hold no one else accountable for any vocal health problems you may encounter. Hurting your voice is purely a self-inflicted injury. With that said, I must admit that I am appalled at some of the poor habits I have seen many vocal teachers and coaches teach. I have had so many students come to me, after studying some of these poorly thought out systems, with the most amazing amount of bad habits. Many of these singers have been taught to push from their support systems. They tend to know little to nothing about how resonance really works. All they usually know about the throat is that they are supposed to relax it, although few of them have any specific idea how to go about doing that. If you've made it this far in *The Art of Body Singing,* then you know full well how big the subjects of "voice assembly" and "voice development" are. Unfortunately, so many contemporary systems, and their teachers, seem to have less to teach than you learned in Volume One of this system alone. Instead, they place their emphasis on so called "performance training" and "interpretation." This is rather a case of putting the cart before the horse. For if you haven't enabled a singer to fully navigate their instrument, how can you ask them to fully navigate their emotions through that instrument? I still maintain that it is your responsibility to search for answers. If a teacher is basically repeating the same lesson over and over, letting you chew up the entire session singing, only to give you a vague analysis at the end of the session, I say, "move on." Also, always remember, "pain is not acceptable." If it hurts to sing, then you are singing incorrectly.

THE INTERNAL TACHOMETER

As you know, the ear is the first part of the voice. It is imperative to teach yourself to listen to how the different switches in your body sound. Every time you access these switches, make an internal note on how they feel. The more developed this sense of feel is, the more equipped you will be to perform in an ensemble situation. The voice is an acoustic instrument, and even when enforced with an electrical PA system is not a match for the louder instruments of the world. The correct answer to this dilemma is arrangement. When a band acknowledges that they must create intelligent arrangements around the vocalist, then that is the beginning to a healthy singing environment. Probably one in a hundred bands you listen to live have successfully achieved this. Even in a well-arranged ensemble the percentage for hearing one's self sing is greatly reduced from the controlled practice room. Many live stages have poor monitoring systems that also help in greatly reducing this percentage. Therefore, it is mandatory that a singer has a well developed *internal tachometer* to prevent oversinging. This is why so much emphasis is placed on taking yourself inside your body as you sing. With your *internal tachometer,* you should virtually be able to sing safely and sound good even when you can't hear yourself at all. Not being able to hear yourself at all would, of course, be a worst case scenario. The more you play live though, the more you will certainly experience poor monitor systems. Earlier I instructed you to keep your tool tape turned down low, so that you could hear yourself perfectly and not oversing. Now is a good time to begin experimenting with raising the volume, so that you can really be sure that you are feeling yourself sing.

VOCAL THERAPY

We have spent a great deal of time learning the healthiest possible approach to High Level singing. Still, it is important to acknowledge a learning curve in fully comprehending these techniques. Also, one must acknowledge that since the voice is basically the body, everyday can be a different challenge with singing. If you are ill or tired, you may not be as in touch with your instrument as you would be on a better physical day. This can leave you vulnerable to improper technique. On these days, my first suggestion is that you warm up as long as it takes to feel the connection with your instrument. Never get into a warm up routine that has a time limit. Listen to your body and always take the necessary steps to be healthy and sound good. With that in mind, I have included one of my favorite vocal therapy exercises, the *taps exercise* (see below), to eliminate and help heal any discomfort you might encounter from poor judgment. You may also use this exercise, along with a few of the lighter exercises from Volume One, as a warm down exercise after an ambitious singing session. It is very common for a singer to experience vocal discomfort the day following a long singing session. This is often a result of not spending a few minutes "warming down." When you sing on a high level for a long period of time (even with the healthiest of techniques), there is a lot of blood concentrated in the muscles in your throat. If this blood stays there as your body cools down, it can cause swelling in these muscles creating discomfort and pressure in the throat. Therefore, a short warm down can help disperse this blood allowing you to start each day on a clean slate.

Chronic vocal problems are typically a result of strain and abuse. The principle disorders range from slightly reddened and/or swollen cords (resulting in chronic laryngitis) to seriously damaged cords. Damaged cords, sometimes called bowed vocal cords, are when the edges of the cords curve concavely allowing too much air to pass through them, resulting in chronic hoarseness or breathiness. Another serious problem is the development of benign growths (vocal nodules and polyps which seem to develop from the cords being irritated by touching each other, due to over-pressurizing and throat constriction.) Healthy cords vibrate slightly apart during phonation. A vocal therapist's prescription is usually a series of exercises to create the same level of relaxation in the throat that we have already worked so hard to achieve in this system.

With this level of relaxation achieved, the voice will usually heal itself and no further action is necessary. In the old days, vocal rest (eliminating singing and often speaking for extended periods of time) was the typical prescription. The problem with that was obvious. Even if the voice healed, it was only a matter of time until it was damaged again because the patient hadn't learned to remedy poor habits. This, too, is often the problem with the more severe prescription of vocal surgery (in the case of growths on the cords). So remember, good habits are just as easy to learn as bad habits. They may cost a little more in the beginning, but they will pay for themselves over and over. If your habits seem to be good and you are still suffering from discomfort in the throat, see a vocal therapist. It may be something unrelated to singing or speaking, or it may be that your habits are not as good as you think.

THE TAPS EXERCISE

Think of this as a little vocal cord massage. In reality, it is a massage of the muscles and tissues directly surrounding the vocal cords. Remember, the vocal cords are not muscles per se. They are commonly termed "mucosa lined membrane." Think of them as thin, flexible, multi-layered ligament/muscle tissue surrounded by the cartilages and the muscles (intrinsic and extrinsic) that make up the larynx. An excellent description of the "anatomy and physiology of the vocal mechanism" is given by David Blair McClosky in his book "Your Voice at its Best," appendix pages 112-128. There is also a useful description of the five layers of the vocal folds given by Robert T. Sataloff in his article "The Human Voice," published in Scientific American, Dec., 1992. When the voice is strained due to oversinging, what tends to happen is that the muscles in and around the larynx tend to spasm, constrict and frog up. When this happens, the vocal chords are greatly restricted in their mobility which can lead to even further complications and disorders. Therefore, it is imperative to remedy the problem before it gets worse.

Listen to example on **Volume Four** recording.

THE ART OF BODY SINGING by BRECK ALAN

One of my all time favorite exercises for this purpose is the *Taps Exercise*. Listen carefully to the example on the Volume Four recording. This is a gentle, little gasping exercise. The little gasp ensures that you are getting a "glottal closure" between each note. This is produced by the closing of the "glottis," the space between the vocal cords, by the intrinsic muscles in the larynx (as opposed to the extrinsic muscles surrounding the larynx that we wish to either completely relax or use for anti constriction purposes). Do not confuse this "glottal closure" with a "glottal stop," which is produced by lifting the back of the tongue to the soft palate as is done when producing the word "king." This "glottal closure" is merely a little gasp which creates and then releases a slight pressure between the vocal cords and the air from the lungs to stimulate the muscles in and around the larynx. An easy way to create this little "gasp" is by holding your breath and releasing small amounts of air directly from the larynx. When you hold your breath the intrinsic muscles and ventricular bands (false cords), constrict inside the larynx to trap air in the lungs. It should be fairly easy to feel yourself release small, gentle "gasps" of air directly from the larynx. Once you can create the "gasp" then add a tone to it, and you have *the Tap's Exercise.*

Use the vowel "i" (ah-e) in your comfortable middle range on a repeated pitch. This is a very little and quiet exercise. Be gentle. If you push this exercise, you will be defeating its purpose. The real key to the *Tap's Exercise* is to hear the little gasp, and to repeat it for two to three minutes. You will achieve the amazing results this exercise is capable of generating. Used properly, the *Tap's Exercise* should eliminate the feelings of fatigue, scorching and strain in your throat associated with misuse and oversinging. Make note that I do not consider this exercise a panacea for misuse of the voice, but instead a very helpful addition to our repertoire of vocal mechanics exercises. Singing is an ongoing pursuit and we should always try and be prepared for the journey. Once repeating this exercise over one pitch is comfortable, try moving it around a bit. It shouldn't be necessary though to move it full range, as the best results are usually achieved in the lower and middle range.

ADDITIONAL THROAT MAINTENANCE

Early signs of "vocal strain" can usually be detected by a tickle in your throat, or by needing to cough frequently during singing. These are usually clear signs that you're singing through your throat. The best way to stop this from happening before it starts is by warming up even better then you currently are. Don't forget the *four parts to a singing session* (1. preliminary warm-up 2. exercise and workout 3. warm-up singing 4. full singing). Following the correct process should definitely help to eliminate vocal strain before it starts.

Coughing and clearing your throat should be done very gently and only when absolutely necessary. The mechanics involved in both of these activities has to do with constricting the throat and forcing out air, to either dislodge matter from the throat or expel it from the lungs. Although these activities might be unavoidable at times, it is imperative that a singer learn to do them with extreme care. The pressure created in the throat (thoracic pressure) for both of these activities can certainly cause strain on the vocal cords. So be gentle.

Dairy products are often considered taboo for singers. This is because they produce mucous which can obstruct the tone passage and even interfere directly with the vocal cords. It is important to remember that the vocal cords are lined in mucous to begin with (although it is a higher quality mucous than is produced elsewhere in the throat and nasal passage). This is for the purpose of keeping them moist and flexible. Therefore, on the subject of addition mucous in the throat and nasal passage caused by dairy products, my advice is to listen to your body. If this additional mucous is dramatically interfering with your singing, then abstain. If even the slightest bit of mucous is interfering in the form of *throat rattle,* then I suggest that you concentrate more on singing *over your throat.*

If your body creates an excess in mucous and it is interfering with your singing, then you might try gargling with a light salt water rinse (use a high quality sea salt as it is much gentler then iodized salt). Be sure and gargle very gently, as forceful gargling can cause the same sort of pressure on your vocal cords as coughing and clearing your throat.

Singing while sick with a seasonal virus (i.e. cold and flu) is a reality for the professional singer. The advice I give here is the same as above, sing *over your throat.* However, if a doctor suggests that you stay in bed then you should follow that advise.

Smoking interferes with your singing in two ways. First, the smoke can dry out the vocal cords, which can, of course, over time cause serious effects. Secondly, smoking can interfere with your lungs ability to be truly "supportive" during vocalization. At any rate, you don't need me to tell you that smoking is bad for you. If you smoke, and that's that, then just be aware of these effects on your singing and listen to your body. If you smoke during performance, and that's that, then keep plenty of water on stage to keep your throat moist.

Coffees and black teas are diuretics and can also dry out your throat. Be moderate with these. Herbal teas are great during singing because the warmth provides a very soothing effect on the throat, and because herbal teas will not dry your throat out nearly as much as black teas. For that matter warm water (perhaps with a slice of lemon in) it is probably the best overall drink during singing. Drinking a lot of water in general is good advice.

As much as alcohol might be inspiring to some people during a performance, I personally do not suggest its use. For one, it tends to impede your judgment which can lead to oversinging. Secondly, it can severely dehydrate your body and dry out your throat. Both undesirable consequences. If drinking during a performance is just something you do, and that's that, then be moderate and keep plenty of water (preferably warm) on stage to keep your throat moist and your body hydrated.

There are several interesting so called remedies in the world for a rough and irritated throat. These range from special coating teas, to aloe gel (which is a naturally, healthy product), to a variety of home remedies. My favorite being fresh ground turmeric, mixed in your palm by the forefinger of your other hand, with unprocessed honey and then placed on the back of your tongue and gently swallowed. This was taught to me by my dear friend Leena Dillingham. If your throat is irritated due to changes in the weather, a cold related virus, or other health related causes, then I recommend that you try these remedies. If the irritation purists, see your doctor. However, if these irritations are directly related to your singing then these remedies will only help cover up a much deeper problem (your improper technique), if they help at all. So, don't be fooled by wonder cures, the cure lies in your ability to keep your throat healthy via good process and mechanics.

TONE BY ATTITUDE

As a former teacher and still good friend of mine (Doug Alexander) used to say, "above all, its got to be entertaining." He was referring to performance in general and I believe he was right. After all, singing is acting. Some manage to overact and some manage to underact. That, I'll leave up to you. But what I would like you to think about at this point, is connecting all of the work we've been doing so far on *tone marriage*, *air ratios*, *energy changes*, *projection values*, etc., to different attitudes and emotions. This is purely experimental and subjective so don't be looking for exacts here. This is what interpretation is all about. Learn your interpretation of an emotion, not mine. One person might sing angry on as loud and hard of a tone as they possibly can, while another may express that anger on an high energy yet airy and fairly quiet, haunting tone giving the impression that explosion is only seconds away.

I'd like you to use the emotions and attitudes listed below to experiment with this subject of *tone by attitude*. Maybe take just one line of a song you know, and sing it over and over playing with various combinations of techniques (i.e. ratios, resonance placement, projection values, energy levels, articulation, etc., etc.) until you feel that you have reached your "interpretation" of the specific emotion or attitude you're working on. Then, just for an exercise, try to lock into that specific attitude for an entire song. Play with this concept of *tone by attitude* thoroughly. The whole idea of this exercise is to heighten your imaginative thought process. Don't worry if it sounds funny or over-acted at first. Simply by experimenting with specific interpretations, you will be cultivating amazing powers for performance when this becomes entirely natural to you. After the initial strangeness of this "acting" exercise wears off, this generally becomes one of the more fun type of sessions you'll experience.

Write the following emotions and attitudes on cue cards and keep them handy for experimentation. After locking into specific attitudes becomes comfortable, begin flashing the cards randomly to see how quickly you can change your tone by attitude. Remember that the random flashing is only a drill and it will generally be more effective to find the few specific emotions or attitudes of a song and then try to stay in character. Keeping this in mind might help prevent the overacting that often accompanies a singer discovering their ability to interpret emotions and attitudes.

Attitudes and Emotions:

Surprised, frightened, ashamed, meek/shy, arrogant, dignified, dry, monotonous, dis passionate/dull, eager, hilarious, amused, accusing, satiric, caressing, forgiving, insane, furious/savage, nervous, sorrowful/sad, annoyed, disgusted, disappointed, regretful, worried/troubled, happy/cheerful/elated, peaceful/satisfied/contented, critical/insinuating, uncertain, sincere, candid/frank, wistful, indignant, explanatory

This list is, of course, small and incomplete. For a more detailed study of interpretation and training in this area I suggest you investigate H. Wesley Balk's books, "The Complete Singer Actor" and "Performing Power, " available from the University of Minnesota Press, Minneapolis 55414.

PLAYING WITH THE DIPHTHONG ON TOP

Here is another tone awareness exercise for high level workouts. Practice your diphthongs ("a" = eh-ee, "i" = ah-ee and "o" = uh-uu) from your middle to your extreme upper range, paying attention to the second vowel in each diphthong. Make sure it doesn't rise up out of your body and resonant entirely in your head. Also, do not allow your throat to close around the second vowel sound and create excessive throat pressure. This should basically be considered another deliberate tone exercise to help you continually develop your sense of mechanics.

THE OLD SCHOOL FLEX

I want to point out that I'm never a proponent of held tension. But High Level singing is such a physical proposition that the concentration required can sometimes really confuse one's body. When you add up all of the things happening at any given time in singing, the thought can be staggering. Hopefully though, through this system you have systematically gained enough coordination to allow all of these components to function together harmoniously. Still, I'd like to introduce something that is often taught in classical singing circles that I personally, still find useful for extremely difficult sections in singing. I call it the *old school flex*. It's basically a way of transferring tension from anywhere in your upper body, to the lower half of your body, by flexing your buttocks all the way down your legs and gripping the ground with your toes. Remember to release the "flex" though, as held tension is very costly in the energy department. Experiment with this technique and I think you'll agree that it truly has its place in extremely difficult singing.

GENTLE REMINDER OF OUR SUPPORT SYSTEM GOALS

Remember that we are attempting to develop a support system that involves the muscles from three or so inches below our naval, up to the diaphragm. We are trying to open up and align our bodies. These muscle groups, that make up our support system, can then work freely on a reflex basis, eliminating the possibility of pushing and shoving. Remember the general rule of thumb, that the lower in your range that you sing, the lower in your support system you use; and the higher in your range that you sing, the higher in your support system you will use. These are general rules, but in a well co-ordinated singer they tend to hold true. Listen to the Volume Four recording for more reasoning on this subject and remember, eighty percent of posture has to do with the support system. So align your body!

DOUBLE HAND TECHNIQUE

Your hands and a mirror can be of great service in your singing progress. The *double hand technique* proves that. While you're practicing your high level singing, simply put one hand flat on your chest, and cup the other hand below your belt line. The hand on your chest will keep you aware of how much vibration is going on in your body. This can be of great service in keeping your tone connected. The hand below your belt line, will help you remember to engage your lower support system muscles. Try it!

HEROES

At this point, it is very important that you have a couple of heroes who are slightly out of your comfort level of singing. You have, by now, acquired enough information in your head and body to break down the mechanics of any singers techniques and successfully navigate their material. It might easily take months per hero, but this is how you will improve by huge strides. Face these challenges and chip away. Make this part of your singing session so that it fits into your routine. Go for it!

(At this point review the end of Volume Two, the *four parts to a singing session*.)

A MODEL TONE EXERCISE FOR SUSTAINED TONE COMBOS

Part two of your singing session is where you will be able to make the most improvement in your technique and mechanical skills. One of the most effective techniques I've found, for practicing the myriad of techniques in singing, is over a *sustained tone combo*. This is where you line up a series of techniques and execute them over one note. With all that you have learned so far, you should be able to invent quite a few combos.

Listen to **Volume Four** recording for example.

The example on the recording starts on a *number three ratio* with *fast air*. Move to a *number one ratio* staying very *anchored* in the *half way technique*, open up with the *percentage technique*, then decrescendo staying on the *number one ratio*, decreasing your energy to achieve the decrescendo. This exercise covers several techniques while staying on one pitch. See how many variations like this one you can invent. This sort of exercise is wonderful for your coordination. It may help to limit yourself to one *sustained tone combo* per session, so that you can completely experience it full range.

THE SANTA HO HO

This exercise is for singers whose middle lower to lower abdominal muscles are not responding well on a reflex basis during singing. I want you to practice this exercise and then forget it. Remember, we're not trying to be pushy, shovey singers. This is just a wake up exercise for some bodies slower to respond to a kinder, gentler approach. In a mirror, watch your lower abdominals move with every note while singing "ho" over the first five notes of the major scale.

ho	ho	ho	ho	ho	ho	ho	ho	ho
do	re	mi	fa	sol	fa	mi	re	do

This should resemble Santa's belly moving while laughing. Use a nice airy ratio to avoid the risk of creating any excess throat pressure. Repeat exercise several times.

CLONING THE TONE

Here's another way to practice staying loyal to a technique, when you desire to stay loyal to a technique. Basically, pick a tone of any flavor and make yourself sing entire sessions on that tone. This is about focus as much as anything else. What's the first thing to guide this exercise? Why, the ear of course.

You can also practice this exercise with *cloning the size*. More than anything this will help you learn to lock into an energy level. Once you can consciously lock into an energy level and stay loyal to it, then changing energies when desired should be well within your grasp.

THROAT EFFECTS

This is the ultimate technique in teaching a singer how to healthily create the edgy, grindy tones most associated with heavy music. These techniques are rarely taught by teachers, because of the extreme difficulty in doing them correctly and healthily. In fact, many teachers of voice will adamantly claim that there is no way to execute these tones with "proper" and "correct" singing technique. Many simply claim that any singer capable of singing with these throaty tones, without hurting themselves, must possess a speaking voice of the same quality. And, while this is true in some cases, it is undoubtedly untrue in most cases. The fact is, that the truly successful "throaty" sounding singers have simply discovered the correct series of mechanics that will allow them to healthily achieve this tone night after night, year after year. It must also be noted that there are several cases of singers that have temporarily or permanently damaged their voices by incorrectly executing these "throaty" tones. Let it also be noted that several opera singers have had very short careers do to damaging their throats with supposedly much "purer" tones. Never underestimate the difficulty of high level singing, be it clean or nasty. All singing must be done with respect to the tiny originators of tone, the vocal cords. Never can you jeopardize the safety of your vocal cords for a particular tone.

So, let me state right now that you must take your own responsibility for practicing these techniques. I will assume no liability, due to the fact that virtually any student who develops vocal disorders, in singing, simply isn't working slowly and deliberately enough. One must carefully repeat "all" of the proper steps to successfully execute the technique being tried. Every technique taught in *The Art of Body Singing* has been well worn by your humble narrator and by many students over the course of many years. These techniques have all been created with the utmost concern for vocal health. Any haste and impatience in singing can immediately set you off on a dangerous path, so I urge you to be prudent.

Throat effects is another intense study in resonance. In fact, I want you to think of *throat effects* as throat resonance. So often we hear in singing, "do not sing in your throat." Well in the areas of excessive *throat pressure* (our goal is always *conversation level throat pressure*) and "articulation" (articulate in your mouth, not in your throat) this statement is correct. However, in the terms of resonance it is short-sighted. Even with the cleanest of tones, we are resonating in our throats. How can we possibly not, considering this is where the tone originates. With *throat effects,* the goal is to place our resonance at specific places in our *tone passage* to create the various "edginess" and "growliness" that can only come from that area. To identify the location of this resonance, you must treat it like a *tone isolation exercise* first (listen to Volume Four recording for example). You can do this by finding a very gentle growl in your throat through a hum. Be gentle. I do not subscribe to a method, taught by some contemporary systems, of deliberately stretching the vocal cords to help achieve manipulated tones from them.

It is my goal with *throat effects* (and any other technique I might be working on), to really work around the cords as much as possible rather than directly manipulating them for supposed quicker results. There is an automatic process in the larynx that changes the length of the cords for pitch variation. I, personally, want to avoid any extra voluntary stretching and manipulation of the cords, as I do not feel that it can be healthy in the long run to do otherwise. So, work your tone (regardless of what type it is) with "resonance placement" and *tone marriage*. That is my advice. *Throat effects* is a technique that will take hard work and patience to properly achieve. If you've made it this far in *The Art of Body Singing,* then that concept won't be new to you. You need to carefully locate this resonance in your throat and "marry" it to the other resonances in your body.

Listen to example on **Volume Four** recording.

The *deep throat growl* is achieved by starting with a very anchored *half way technique,* and adding *throat resonance* to the top of it. In effect, the *throat resonance* replaces much or all of the *nasal horn resonance* (depending on your taste and skill level). The *throat resonance* becomes the projecting resonance of the *tone marriage. Projection value* is certainly one of the biggest reasons heavy singers gravitate to the *throat resonances.* It is a tone that will literally cut through the thickness of loud music. its edginess can also give the illusion of aggressiveness associated with screaming. But it is not screaming, it is projecting. And, it can be learned by anyone with the patience to put the pieces together. When doing the *deep throat growl* stay very, very *anchored.* This will keep you from singing *through your throat.* If you are feeling any constriction resulting in over-pressurization in the throat, back off. This means you haven't found the technique yet. Remember, this is just another switch, but you have to locate it and master turning it on. Start in your middle range, be as gentle and as quiet as possible. Once you master the switch, you can practice this technique full range and with varying energy levels.

The *edgy soft palate grind* starts from the *nasal horn* and adds the *throat resonance* from the soft palate on down. This will be a brighter, grindier *throat resonance.* Once you can thoroughly use this technique, begin to add lower resonances to warm it up (if desired). Some singers have more luck at first with one or the other of these *throat effects.* See what works for you and then begin to experiment with others. The smoky, grainy tone a lot of singers get can be achieved by using an airier ratio and adding some soft pallet resonance to it. Play with them all, but always take your time and be safe.

These are amazing techniques when done correctly. Always think "open" with your throat when attempting *throat effects* (and any other singing, of course). Do not constrict your throat. If you do, the result will be a "gargling" sort of effect and will lead to excessive *throat pressure.* The biggest problem singers run into, when attempting to master *throat effects* too quickly, is to forget their good habits in singing. *Throat effects* is not a foreign, outlandish concept, but instead another mechanics technique to broaden your singing horizons. Practice this technique in small doses. It will come to you a little at a time. It will not be unusual for the already advanced singer to spend one to two years navigating *throat effects* properly. If you are in a hurry this is the wrong technique for you to try. So be responsible.

CONCLUSION OF VOLUME FOUR

I would like to congratulate you for making it this far with *The Art of Body Singing.* I am aware of the amount of work required to get to this point. Hopefully, you have taken your time and really absorbed each subject. Perhaps now, you should work for awhile on the techniques and concepts that have stuck to you so far. I would certainly suggest that in the future you review and re-study the entire system. You'll be amazed at how much the review will help, once a great portion of the material has really settled into you. The glossary at the end of Volume Four, should also prove to be a wonderful periodic refresher and study guide. If you are a teacher and you wish to teach these techniques, I ask only that you teach them responsibly. Just as the first part of the voice is the ear, so is the first part of being a voice teacher. It is imperative that a teacher be able to identify the mechanical habits of a singer by listening. To do this, you must truly understand all of these techniques for what they are: tools. They are tools to assemble and develop a high quality instrument. They have been taught in a responsible order, so that a student might really be prepared for each stage of growth. Never skip ahead in your own studies or in teaching others this highly detailed instrument. I've said it to many students in my life and I'll say it to you, "the slow way is the fast way." Be deliberate with things of this nature and your growth will know no bounds.

I wish you well and hope that we shall cross paths again in the future.

Breck Alan

Please visit Bodysinging.com to purchase easy to follow routine CDs of the exercises contained in this book.

NOTES
FROM THE AUTHOR

Let me first just say that I never set out to be a teacher. I took classes at various music schools and colleges around the world, as well as studying privately with a plethora of teachers for one reason: to learn what I needed to be a more productive singer. The problem was that when it came to vocal mechanics, that was no easy feat. Looking back, it still amazes me that so many teachers had so few tools, when it came to teaching vocal mechanics. It never seemed to take very long to expire a teacher of their knowledge of the specifics of the voice. I guess the only reason I felt I needed so many specifics, was that I never felt that I could cover all of the ground I wanted to cover with my singing. The things I had learned about it, hadn't taught me to continue my growth. So, consequently, I was always in search of more information that made sense to me. I was always experimenting with my own voice, just trying to do what every singer really wants to do, sound good to their own ear. I could never tell anyone that I haven't been strongly influenced by the world of information that exists on this subject called "Voice". What I can honestly say is that I feel *The Art of Body Singing* has fine tuned and organized the bits and pieces I picked up in one place or another. With some of it I got lucky and discovered on my own during my late night practice sessions over the last twenty years. If I thought there was anything like this system of vocal mechanics training anywhere in the world, I can promise you that I would have bought it myself and surely not spent the five gillion hours producing this one. Although make no mistake, producing this system has been much like the entire journey of singing, a labor of love.

I owe, and am indebted for help along my vocal journey to many. A few of whom are Steve Heck and Peter Elvins for their huge patience in finally getting me to work hard enough to find my voice. To Richard Schumacher, Doug Alexander, Ran Blake and Don Rendal for their tenacity and insights in making me work my inner ear. To a myriad of other music teachers and musicians that I've been lucky enough to work with along the way who encouraged and inspired me. To Robert Cord, for rewarding me time and time again with praise, when I felt so overworked and underloved during my intense study years in Boston. To Joseph Nolan, for helping me build a vocal booth in my apartment in Boston, so that I could practice at all hours of the night without bothering my roommates, Laura and Kathleen. To Bob Minor, for the high praise of the first version of this project, and for encouraging me to finish this version. To every single one of the many students that I have been fortunate enough to work with, for it was only through working with this myriad of students (every one of them different) that I have been able to structure and fine tune *The Art of Body Singing*. And to Marina C. who told me once that all of my experiences good and bad would be portrayed in my singing, and I always thought that was a cool thing to say.

I must also credit here some of the vocal instruction publications that have strongly impressed and influenced me over the years. For starters, the first book about voice that I ever read was P. Mario Marafioti's "Caruso's Method of Voice Production" from Dover Press. This book had a profound influence over me and I still think its incredible. Another book that I've gained much pleasure from over the course of many years is "Your Voice at its Best" by David Blair McClosky. Mr. McClosky was a vocal therapist for many years in New England and has strongly influenced that field. His books are available through

The Boston Music Company, 172 Tremont St., Boston, MA 02111. I also greatly enjoyed Alan Green's book, "The New Voice," largely because he spends the majority of the book dealing with matters concerning throat mechanics (a typically glossed over subject). Mr. Green's book is available through Hal Leonard Publishing.   For matters concerning music interpretation, I strongly suggest H. Wesley Balk's books "The Complete Singer Actor" and "Performance Power" (available through University of Minnesota Press, Minneapolis 55414) and as a guide to diction I suggest "The Singers Manual of English Diction" by Madeleine Marshall (available on Schirmer Books). I must also say that I greatly admire Seth Riggs for his fresh ideas and huge influence on modern voice teaching.

Since finishing the writings in this book I have discovered the writings of Lamperti and hope that I can say with all humility that he is a kindred spirit of mine. After you've worked your way through "The Art of Body Singing" check out Vocal Wisdom by Giovanni Battista Lamperti from Taplinger Publishing. its beauty really shines once your sense of vocal mechanics is established.

Have fun,

Glossary

Adam's Apple: The front of your larynx. Technically your thyroid cartilage.

Adjusting on the Fly: An absolute necessity in performance to ensure that you maintain a continuous rather than a clunky and indecisive energy.

Air Spigot: The imagery of the control valve for the support system.

Anchoring: The art of placing your resonance at the nasal passage as an aid to control throat pressure and avoid oversinging. This should also be considered the beginning sound board for all resonance.

Anti-Constrictor Muscles: The muscles used in and around the throat (including the tongue) to drop the larynx, groove the tongue and open the throat.

Art of Body Singing: The system of vocal training which teaches you to intelligently navigate all of the components of the voice, guides you in the process of assembling and using your high quality instrument (voice), and prepares you for continued growth in singing and performance.

Assembly: The process of coordinating vocal techniques from actual vocal mechanics.

Auto Pilot Singing: Singing without the singer considering him/herself part of the audience. In other words, a singer that isn't listening to him/herself.

Back off: The thing singers guilty of oversinging have to constantly remind themselves to do. Big singing is done successfully by coordination, not bullying.

Backwards Into the Body: The art of singing behind and over the throat, using resonance to achieve size and color rather than force.

Belting Principle of Centering the Tone: Learning to eliminate the ease in, and attack the note in its center. This increases projection value and gives the illusion of belting.

Blending: A common term for connecting the resonance chambers into a balanced tone. In this system we refer to blending as tone marriage, tone harmony and circle of tone.

Bottle Necking: Forcing too much air through the throat.

Bright Tone: 1. The result of singing a light, released tone (see throat pressure) and possibly singing through the mouth horn (see resonance). 2. The result of using the edgy overtones produced by the nasal horn to increase projection value (also see resonance).

Buffer Air: The airiness on top of the tone that acts as a release of throat pressure.

Bully: Something you can not successfully be with your voice. The voice is a democracy of all its components.

Buzzy: Also called edgy, this is the resonance produced by the nasal horn.

The Candle Theory: The theory that states that no matter how big, or loud, or airy, or aggressive you may be singing, never should you be able to blow out a small candle placed in front of your mouth. Slightly flicker the candle, but never blow it out. Use your fingers as a gauge, not a candle.

Centering the Pitch: An exercise designed to help tune the ear for the result of having good intonation (being in tune).

Cloning the Tone: Staying loyal to a set tone for an extended period, for the purpose of mastering the techniques necessary to create that tone.

Closed Nasal Technique: Closing the nasal passage, resulting in a stuffy nose sound. This is a remarkable aid in learning to anchor your sound and not sing through the throat.

Clunkiness: Moving through the mechanics of voice in a not so seamless manner.

Coach: A provider of encouragement and generalisms. (as opposed to Teacher)

Connecting the Dots: The image of connecting the "four parts of the voice" in a balanced democracy.

Conscious Relaxation: The art of taking your awareness inside your throat and relaxing.

Constrictor Muscles: The muscles in the throat involved in swallowing and closing. One of the first things a singer must learn to do is identify and relax these muscles.

Continuous Energy: We don't sing notes, we sing phrases. You must supply continuous energy to a phrase to give it life. Do not ration your energy.

Conversation Level Throat Pressure: The perfect level of healthy throat pressure, that should never be exceeded regardless of size or energy level of singing.

Crescendo: A dynamic change from softest to loudest.

Deceptive Air: See fast air.

Decrescendo: A dynamic change from loudest to softest.

Diction: In this system we stress skipping off the consonant and living on the vowel. More specifics are certainly mentioned in each volume but an extensive study of diction with a dedicated diction manual is suggested.

Diphthong: A sound composed of two consecutive vowel sounds in the same syllable.

Double Hand Technique: One hand on the chest to be constantly in touch with the resonance being produced there, and the other hand on the lower abdominals to gently remind (not push) them to stay awake.

Drool Exercise: The exercise in which we learn to relax so effectively in and around the throat, that we kick in the salivatory glands.

Dropped Larynx Technique: Using the anti-constrictor muscles in the throat to drop the larynx, this technique is used to both change the shape of this area in the throat (different shape equals different tonal characteristics), and to help with placing chest resonance.

Dynamic Breathing: Developing a sense of dynamic range (from the quietest and softest to the loudest and hardest) in your singing. This is achieved not only with a good sense of singing mechanics, but also with good grasp of energy changes.

Ease In and Ease Out Techniques: The art of eliminating the clunkiness often associated with entering and exiting a note by easing in and easing out.

Ease: The state of being a singer should be in, while learning to coordinate the first two volumes of The Art of Body Singing.

Energy Air: See fast air.

Energy: A wonderful, variable, necessary part of singing.

Entries: Entering a note.

Exaggeration: A necessity in the practice room in order to thoroughly discover the instrument.

Experimenting: Something of paramount importance in truly navigating the mechanics of the voice. Experimenting though, without good guidance from a good mechanics teacher typically leads to a plethora of bad and unhealthy singing habits.

Extreme Reverse Resonance Exercise: An exercise where you practice pulling your resonance in the opposite direction from which the pitch is traveling.

Falsetto Principles: 1. In this system falsetto is described as the tone created by singing through the mouth horn. 2. The light, bright voice produced by disconnecting and releasing from the chest and nasal horn resonance chambers and singing exclusively in the mouth horn.

Fast Air: The technique designed to increase the level of energy (air) in singing without increasing throat pressure

Fast Air Crescendos: This technique involves a ratio shift from a number three ratio with fast air energy to a number one ratio, without changing the energy. This should produce the largest possible size in your tone.

Feel: One part of singing that makes the journey so fun is feeling all of the components of the voice in your body at work together. This is not about manipulation, but about awareness.

Finishing Out: The term used for intentionally or unintentionally withdrawing from an isolated tone.

The Four Parts to a Singing Session: Preliminary warm-up, exercise/workout period, warm-up singing, full singing.

The Fluttering Exercise: The exercise used for centering the pitch.

Flowering: The effect of tone marriage taking shape and increasing your circle of tone.

Freedom: A result of being open.

Grooved Tongue Position: Lying the tongue flat on the floor of the mouth and grooving it so that the tone passage is unobstructed to the exit of the mouth.

Growth: The thing that happens when one stays "open" and nurses one's talents on an ongoing basis.

Gushing: A random release of air during phonation.

Half Way Technique: The beginning of tone marriage, this technique combines the advantages of anchoring with the closed nasal technique, along with adding body to your sound with the chest tone.

Heroes: The singers that should be slightly out of your reach, and therefore inspire you to keep raising the height of the bar during your workouts.

High Sigh: A tone isolation exercise focusing on the mouth horn while swooping downward from the upper range to the lower range.

Inner Ear: The first part of the voice, this is your guide to good musicianship (i.e. pitch, note choice, rhythm etc.) and instrument specific recognition (i.e. tone, inflection, volume, attitude, etc.).

Inside Your Body: Where the mechanics of your instrument live, and therefore where you must take your sensibilities so that you may feel these mechanics at work.

Internal Tachometer: The gauge connected to the series of singing mechanics that prevents you from oversinging even when you're not hearing yourself on the level you might like to.

Interpretation: The art of finding the right colors in your tone and expression to sell the meaning of whatever you are singing. Singing is after all, a form of acting.

Intonation: The result of an instrument being in tune when played.

Journey: Something you must be willing to take if you are serious about finding "your voice."

Kick Start Technique: The technique where the hands are cupped three or four inches below the naval to gentle stimulate the lower abdominal muscles during the "Way Down Exercise."

Larynx: The temple of the vocal cords.

Learning Curve: Something you should expect to encounter before the high level singing techniques taught in this system become natural.

Looping: The wonderful technique of repeating a small section of something over and over until it is right before moving on.

Magic Wand: The thing most singers wish I had so they wouldn't have to practice. One session, $5,000, good-bye.

Masque: See open nasal anchor in this glossary.

Mechanical Switch: Often referred to in this system as switches, and turning on the switches. These are the mechanics of your instrument that you must learn to turn on and develop in your warm-up and vocal workout so that they are available to you during singing.

Minimal Mouth Movement: The art of learning to articulate first inside your mouth with the help of your ear. Excessive mouth movement leads to tension.

Mirror: The thing that can save you a lot of time in learning vocal technique.

The Mixo Exercise: An endurance exercise used with the lip roll.

Mouth Sizing: A common sense technique of opening your mouth wider (still using the singer's smile) as the energy level (air level) increases.

Multi-Register Singing: An obvious breaking of registers as the pitch moves from one area of a singers range to another. Your first goal in this system is one register singing. Then, if you choose to break registers for reasons of interpretation, it will be from choice, not default.

Muscle Memory Singing: The result of typical voice coaching and learning via imitation as opposed to learning via mechanics training. This is the sort of singing that sounds the same on every song regardless of the song's meaning or intention.

Nasal Horn Buzz: The tone isolation exercise used to place resonance deeper and deeper into the nasal horn by maintaining a very open nasal passage.

Naturalization: One of the first keys in stripping away old singy habits and cultivating a new foundation from which to grow. A good place to start is with speaking the melody.

No Black Sheep Rule: The art of listening to your practice so that complete control and evenness of your exercises can be attained. From that foundation, more expressive unevenness in singing will be within your grasp.

No Note District: The complete bottom or top of one's singing range.

Number Two Crescendos: Crescendos done from start to finish on a number two ratio. This requires a good sense of energy changes.

Old School Flex: The endearing technique taught in days of old to flex your buttocks while singing extremely difficult passages. As strange as it may be, it has its place.

Olympic Level Singing: The high level, high energy singing that ambitious singers aspire to.

One Breath Exercise: A tone exercise used for endurance and distance training (the notes being at different distances apart).

One Register Singing: The art of keeping the tone connected while singing throughout your range (as opposed to multi-register singing).

Open Body Vibrato: Open body vibrato is the result of balancing the echoing between the resonance chambers, the evenness of the support system and the perfect level of throat pressure.

Open Nasal Anchor: The nasal passage (where the uvula lives) is the first place the air and initial tone from the vocal cords make contact. By centering (placing) the beginning of resonance here, we can control the pressure in the throat and begin the flowering process of tone marriage. "LET THE BUZZ BE THE GUIDE." This is what is referred to in classical teaching as singing in the "masque".

Open Rib Cage Technique: This technique involves keeping your sternum high and your rib cage open with the aid of the "intercostal muscles" during singing.

Open: Open body, open throat, open mind.

Overcompensating: Using too much air to "reach" a note (usually most apparent in the upper range) resulting in oversinging.

Overpressurizing: What happens in the throat when constriction and pushing are the habits of a singer.

Oversinging: A product of trying to "bully" singing rather than coordinate it. The result is poor tone quality and vocal strain.

Overtones: Sometimes called harmonics, these are the series of tones that effectively harmonize with the fundamental tone being produced. These overtones are what gives each instrument its unique color and quality (timbre).

Percentage Technique: This involves opening up the nasal passage while practicing the half way technique to finish off the circle of tone.

Phonation: Producing sound with the voice.

Ping Pong Exercise: An exercise used first for ear training, and secondly as a distance exercise for singing.

Po Pa Exercise: A high energy distance exercise taught in volume three.

Posture: Posture is about aligning and freeing up your body so that it may contribute to, rather than hinder, your singing.

Potential: Whatever you're willing to make it.

Practice: Often referred to as "wood shedding" by musicians, this slight inconvenience will only entirely determine your success in this (and just about any other) field.

Professional: Officially someone who gets paid for what they do, but realistically one who aspires to the attitude and competence of professionalism.

Projection: For your singing to literally fly from your mouth and body to the listener.

Pulsing Projection: An emphasis exercise designed to give life and expression to your singing performance.

Ratios: See three air ratios.

Ratio Shifting: The practice of shifting seamlessly from one ratio to another.

Rationing: Supplying your singing with rations of support rather than continuous energy.

Resonance: The sympathetic vibration of your body to the tiny vibrations that begin in the throat.

Resonance Follows Pitch: During auto pilot singing your resonance placement will automatically follow your pitch around like a little puppy (i.e. when you're singing in your upper range the resonance will be up in your head, and when you're singing in your lower range the resonance will be in down in your body). The result of this is multi register singing.

Resonance Placement: Placement is often described as "placing your resonance in your head or chest, etc. To me, the key placement is the "anchor". After that it's really about opening up and attaching the other resonances in your body to this.

Resonance Shifting: The exercise of vertically shifting from one resonance chamber to another (mouth horn to chest, back to mouth horn, then into the nasal horn and back to mouth horn).

Reverse Resonance Psychology: The practice of pulling back and down with your resonance placement as you ascend in pitch, and pulling up with your resonance placement as you descend in pitch.

Routine: The methodical series of events that should warm you up, work you out, and put you on the path to continued growth.

Rushing the Tone: Singing through the throat as a result of not having the patience to sing backwards into the body to rely on resonance for size and color.

Santa Ho Ho: An exercise to stimulate the lower abdominal muscles into action. After these muscles have begun to respond it is important to work back towards using them on a reflex basis.

Scorching: A burning irritation in the throat associated with oversinging.

Scratch Tape: A tape used to listen back to yourself practicing exercises and singing.

Set-up: 1. The physical feelings you should teach yourself to feel inside your body before phonation begins. 2. The feelings you must feel in the throat before attacking a note without the ease-in technique.

Settling: That period when all things learned must settle into your mind, body and spirit so that they might surface in a usable form.

Seven Points of Relaxation: Down the face, jaw hinge, stretch jaw, root of tongue, horizontal larynx, back of head and neck, shoulders.

Silent Singing: Just that, singing in your mind.

Singer Release: This effect is achieved by releasing into the mouth horn from a more connected tone.

Singer's Smile: The shaping of the mouth into a slight smile to create a slightly larger exit for cleaner purer articulation.

Singing an Octave Below the Melody: A good way to work your bottom range, wake up your ear and possibly help sing in a relaxed manner in the car.

Singing Backwards Into Your Body: The art of singing behind your throat and using resonance, support and good anchoring instead of force to achieve high level singing.

Singing Behind Your Throat: The art of singing with the perfect level of throat pressure. This is sometimes referred to as singing over your throat.

Singing Off the Breath: Never holding your breath before beginning to sing. This principle also applies to not allowing yourself to constrict in the throat should support begin to diminish.

Singing Through the Throat: The act of creating too much throat pressure (over-pressurization) from either constricting in the throat, pushing with the support system, or not anchoring well.

Singy: The weird singing quality many singers possess when trying to sing beyond their capabilities before learning to do so. This often involves trying to imitate opera singers or pop singers, the result being one of a comic nature.

Siren: A swooping, ascending exercise, staying locked into the half way technique.

Speaking the Melody: The technique that should teach you to clearly understand the connection between singing and speaking.

Strain: A product of oversinging.

Student: Anyone hungry to learn something and willing to go through the necessary steps to reach that goal.

Style: Ideally, the reflection of the individual's personality and life experience, which should be thoroughly enhanced (not manipulated) through vocal training.

Support System: All that is connected with breath control in singing.

Supposedly Tone Deaf: Although I'm sure it's possible that a physical or psychological defect in a small percentage of people might cause the disability to discern and match pitches, In all of my cases I have never seen this to be so. People who cannot match pitches simply need to be taught to do so in a gentle methodical manner (see Volume One "Before We Get Started").

Sustain: To hold a note (on a vowel or musical consonant) for a duration longer than is done during speaking. In fact sustaining is the first departure from speaking into singing.

Sustained Tone Combos: A good way to practice sustained tones while changing through a variety mechanical techniques.

System: An organized methodology for learning anything.

Tangible: That which we can really learn to identify, hear, feel and often see, as opposed to the pure imagery that is so often used in teaching this instrument. Certainly not to suggest that all imagery is useless.

Taps Exercise: A light vocal cord massage used for light rehabilitation of vocal strain and as a wonderful warm down.

Teacher: A provider of realism and hard cold facts, while maintaining the insights to help a student find his/her individual path.

Tessetura: The part of the singing range (middle), which produces the highest quality level for the least amount of effort.

Thoracic Pressure: The valvular process of constricting within the larynx to trap air in the lungs. This is done with the aid of the intrinsic muscles of the larynx and the ventricular bands (often referred to as "false vocal chords").

Three Air Ratios: The subject that not only allows us to understand how air works under the tone, but on top of the tone as well. Also a wonderful tool for understanding throat pressure.

Three Parts to a Note: The beginning, the middle and the end. Practicing the ease in and ease out techniques is a good way to truly understand the three parts to a note and to eliminate clunkiness in singing.

Three Resonance Chambers: Chest, mouth horn and nasal horn.

Three Steps to Working Out a Difficult Passage: Happy throat, placement, size.

Three Ways to Crescendo: Shift towards a less airy ratio, increase your energy level, increase your circle of tone.

Throat: This is where everything begins in singing. Although the voice is a democracy of its four components (inner ear, throat, support system and resonance) great reverence must be paid to this part of your instrument to maintain good vocal health and good tone.

Throat Effects: The technique used to healthily create those tones ranging from the lightly smoky to the heavily grindy.

Throat Management: The art of relaxing the constrictor muscles, using the anti-constrictor muscles correctly and monitoring throat pressure.

Throat Pressure: The pressure created between the vocal cords and the respiratory system during phonation.

Throat Rattle or Throat Distortion: The rattling of phlegm in the throat as a result of singing through the throat as opposed to singing over and behind the throat.

Tone by Attitude: A performance exercise designed to help you connect the various tones you've been working on with various attitudes and emotions.

Tone Isolation Exercises: Isolating your resonance in one resonance chamber at a time.

Tone Marriage: Also referred to as tone harmony and circle of tone, this is the art of uniting the resonance chambers to create a whole (tone) larger than the sum of its parts.

Tone Passage: The passage in the throat from where voice begins (vocal cords) to where it exits (the mouth and nasal passage). This is technically referred to as the Pharynx.

Tone Variety: The art of tapping into different tones as they relate to the interpretation of singing.

Tongue Roll and Lip Roll Exercises: Wonderful mechanics exercises taught in this system to teach you to sing behind the pressure created by rolling the tongue or lips, instead of through that pressure. Also wonderful exercises for developing the air spigot in the support system.

Tongue Roll Mm Ah and Lip Roll Mm Ah Exercises: The mechanical exercises designed to help you coordinate the transition from the Tongue Roll or Lip Roll, to a hum and then to an open vowel tone.

Tool Songs: Memorized songs of the appropriate difficulty level for a singer to practice various techniques over.

Triphthong: Three connected vowel sounds.

Two Parts to the Middle: The technique of changing your tone in the middle of a vowel as a highlight or expression.

Under Compensating: Using too little air to reach a note (common in both upper and lower ranges) resulting in tone loss or throat constriction.

Unfinished Tone: Another term for an isolated tone.

Upper Middle: The area in your singing range above a typical singers vocal break. This is the most projecting area of your range, and typically the most difficult to convincingly develop.

Uvula: The cone shaped projection hanging above the back of the tongue. The uvula is a good guide when learning to switch back and forth from an open to closed nasal passage. When the uvula is low the nasopharynx (which leads into the nasal passage) is open. When the uvula is high this passage is closed.

Vertical Resonance: Before you can successfully navigate the art of tone marriage you should be able to place your resonance in each resonance chamber individually (moving up and down). This is referred to as thinking vertically in your resonance.

Vibrato Principles: Open body vibrato is the goal in this system. See open body vibrato in this glossary.

Vocabulary: Officially "all of the words of a language." The Art of Body Singing was designed using as much everyday language as possible to articulate the specific world of voice training.

Vocal Break: Generally the result of disconnecting from the resonance chambers that produce the most size and volume (chest and nasal horn) and releasing into the mouth horn.

Vocal Cords: Coupled with air from the support system, the tiny vibrations started by the vocal cords (also called vocal folds) are where it all begins in singing.

28 Jan 07 Tom Lee

Vocal Disorders: A direct result of over-pressurization in the throat.

Vocal Fatigue: The result of overpressurizing the vocal cords and larynx, resulting in a weak and tired voice.

Vocal Hygiene: The art of maintaining a healthy singing voice at all times.

Vocal Mechanics: All of the tangible physical components of the voice (i.e.. throat, support system and resonance, which are of course guided by the ear).

Vocal Techniques: The skills required to fluidly and consistently navigate the mechanics of the voice.

Vocal Therapy: The various procedures used to correct vocal disorders due to oversinging. Everything about The Art of Body Singing teaches prevention of vocal disorders so that correction and therapy should, hopefully, never be needed.

Volume Diamond: There is a place in your middle range that will produce your loudest singing volume. From that point the volume will taper in both directions. Projection can, however, effectively disguise that tapering.

Warm-up: An imperative for the healthy, professional singer. This is how we turn on all of the mechanical switches for our voice so that they are available to us during singing.

Warming Down: A good idea after high level singing to prevent swelling in the throat due to the high blood circulation created in that area.

Wave of Energy: The imagery used to describe the energy in singing as a wave leaving the entire body, and the notes and words as ships on top of that wave.

Way Down Exercise: The exercise that helps us focus on using our lower support system, begin the process of singing in our lower range, and maintain our big body posture.

Work Out: The part of the singing session that yields the highest level warm-up as well as the highest level of growth.

Yawning the Adam's Apple Down: An often taught exercise to teach singers to drop the larynx.